MW00622690

Title: *Pack Light: A Journey to Find Myself*
Author: Shilletha Curtis
Imprint: Andscape Books
In-store date: 5/21/24
ISBN: 978-1-368-09469-6
Price: US 27.99 / CAN 36.99
E-book ISBN: 978-1-368-09472-6
Trim size: 6 x 9
Page count: 256

ATTENTION, READER:
This is an uncorrected galley proof. It is not a finished book
and is not expected to look like one. Errors in spelling,
page length, format, etc. will be corrected when the book is
published several months from now. Direct quotes should
be checked against the final printed book.

We are pleased to send this book for review.
Please send two copies of any review or mention to:

Disney Publishing Group
Attn: Adult Publicity Department
77 West 66th Street, 3rd Floor
New York, NY 10023
dpw.publicity@disney.com

PACK LIGHT

A JOURNEY TO FIND MYSELF

SHILLETHA CURTIS

ANDSCAPE

LOS ANGELES   NEW YORK

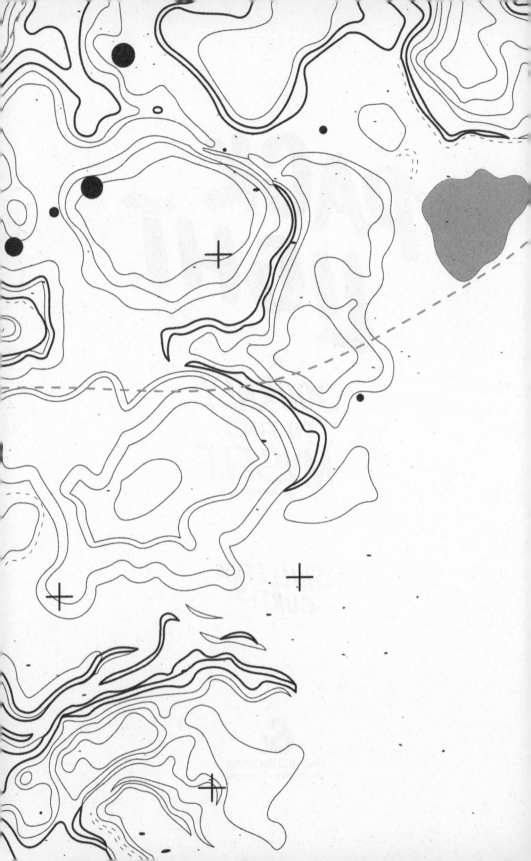

Certain names, locations, identifying characteristics,
and details have been partially altered or withheld
to preserve the privacy of some individuals.

Copyright © 2024 by Shilletha Curtis

All rights reserved. Published by Andscape Books, an imprint of
Buena Vista Books, Inc. No part of this book may be reproduced or
transmitted in any form or by any means, electronic or mechanical,
including photocopying, recording, or by any information storage and
retrieval system, without written permission from the publisher.
For information address Andscape Books,
77 West 66th Street, New York, New York 10023.

First Edition, April 2024
10 9 8 7 6 5 4 3 2 1
FAC-004510-24088
Printed in the United States of America

This book is set in Chaparral Pro/Adobe Originals
Hand lettering by Emmanuel Adjei
Art by Shutterstock
Designed by Stephanie Sumulong

Library of Congress Cataloging-in-Publication Control Number:
2023945403
ISBN 978-1-368-09469-6
Reinforced binding

www.AndscapeBooks.com

CONTENTS

PROLOGUE

When the COVID-19 pandemic came upon the planet, we were forced to lock down like prisoners, trapped in our separate realities that we created for ourselves. Our worlds, structured by our jobs, careers, and responsibilities, halted as the earth stood completely still. Our governments failed us. Bodies piled up. As the pandemic raged, as it stole thousands of lives, I felt its fury each day.

For years, patients of all species—dogs, cats, birds, rabbits, ferrets, and amphibians—came to me every day and entrusted me with their safety and well-being. Loving animals and providing them with medical care brought me peace. My dream and purpose in life, as I knew it then, was to be a vet tech: go to school, get licensed, specialize, and spend my life committed to animals in someplace frigid like Canada. Instead, in reality, I was struggling to hold on to the hat I had so desperately sought to wear since childhood. The pressure of the job was becoming unbearable. Seeing animals as I helped them cross over the rainbow bridge brought bags under my eyes and constant turning and tossing under my covers in the dead of night as I sobbed and cuddled my own dog. Anxiety beat me up like a bully with an insatiable urge for violence, jab after jab, taunt after taunt. I never felt smart enough to be in a field where math determined everything; I could barely read a ruler. Despite pressing on to be what I thought I was destined to be, fear had reached its prongs deep inside my brain. I was afraid of the scars of my past, afraid to break out of the mold, afraid to be myself, afraid to stand in my truth.

In the middle of an already looming crisis, one phone call changed everything.

"Hello, Shilletha. We wanted to inform you that we will be closing the business."

"W-what—?" I stammered.

"We're sorry. It's not just you, it's everyone."

Silence echoed through the phone. I faded into the void. I sat down on my navy-blue comforter decorated with ship anchors, tossed about on the sea without a lifejacket. I surrendered to the tides, drowning in self-pity. I let my tear-filled eyes become accustomed to the darkness as light faded. I had to decide between cruelty or kindness, and cruelty won. Blood had to be shed, for the cross to bear was mine. I begged to feel alive as numbness overcame me.

I fixated on the bathroom door. I rummaged through the drawers and pulled out a white-and-orange razor. I used a lighter to burn the plastic to reveal the meat of the blade inside. Panic switched off my brain; I was no longer me. I was an avatar of the woman inside. My steps, not mine, led me to my car, where the bloodshed began. The one-inch silver razor blade lay in the palm of my left hand, and in my right was my smartphone. Relapse was on the horizon, but help was in the power of my hand.

With all the strength and will to live left within me, I texted my therapist: *I want to die. I am going to cut myself. I lost my job, and I don't know what to do anymore. There is nothing left for me.*

Ping! My phone chimed, and I glanced down. Concerned about my safety, my therapist had responded that she would notify the cops. My stomach dropped. Cops terrified me. They were the enemy to Black folks and only served the white and wealthy. I knew what they were capable of. They had the power to kill without consequences, and the mentally ill were not an exception. Fight-or-flight kicked in, and I weighed my options: Run, possibly be fatally shot, and no justice would be served; or I could sit in my car and comply with the officers' requests. I chose to comply.

Sirens screamed as I cut my wrist three times. One because I was a failure. Two because I was worthless. And three because I didn't deserve to live. Before I could beat myself into a pulp, the cops showed up, and I hid the razor.

"Ms. Curtis, is that you?" the officer said. Great. Another old white man.

My legs trembled at the sound of his voice. "Yes, that's me." I sighed. *Fuck me.*

"We heard you have been having a little bit of trouble. Will you come with us?"

"Yeah . . . I guess." I looked at the white screen door of the house and saw my roommate peering out. *Oh great. This is embarrassing.*

I got out of my car as they searched it for the razor but had no luck. A paramedic who was parked at the end of the U-shaped driveway approached me.

"Ms. Curtis? You ready to go? I'll buckle you in and take some vitals, okay? It should be a quick ride to the hospital."

I nodded, still in shock.

The sliding glass hospital doors hissed as they gave way to sterile white walls that enveloped me. I was led past the registrar's office and into a room with translucent walls and a single white hospital bed. A woman was posted up in a flimsy chair outside the room. She watched me. Suicide watch required such vigilance; not only was I subjected to extreme boredom, so was she. No magazines, phones, or distractions for her.

A technician came into the room, told me to change into sleazy blue hospital scrubs, and warned me that he would be back for blood and a urine sample. I was handed a six-ounce cup with a yellow plastic lid, but I was not granted permission to pee out of sight of the watcher who guarded my cell. Bladder shyness inhibited my ability to relieve myself, and what a pity for the watcher. I rebelled and refused to urinate for two hours unless I could close the curtains and cover my bare ass. Finally the technician obliged, seeing that I had done nothing except hang upside down off the hospital bed and yawn frequently. With the urine sample collected, the psychiatrist appeared and relayed that he had spoken with my therapist.

"Your therapist said you just lost your job, so you're going through a rough patch. Do you feel safe enough to go home and do group therapy through the phone, or would you rather be hospitalized?"

That was simple. I had no interest in being hospitalized. Freedom was a meticulous seesaw, teetering up and down; if I rocked it too much, I would find myself trapped in the mud, and I knew from experience what that was like. I had to break out and run toward freedom.

"I'd rather do outpatient," I said.

I was relieved to be discharged, but I soon found myself back at home, with the walls closing in once again. I attended a virtual group four days a week, but that proved to be unhelpful, as I could not physically interact with others. One spring day, my girlfriend at the time and I decided to leave New Jersey to get out of the city for a hike. Arriving at Harriman State Park in New York, we jumped out of my old silver Nissan Sentra and headed for the trees, eager for a day in the calm woods.

At the foot of a slope, an older white gentleman appeared. After greeting us, he asked, "Have you been out here before?"

We both shook our heads.

"Right behind me is the Appalachian Trail," he said, pointing to a narrow path. He took our blank stares as an invitation to tell us more. "It's one of the longest hiking trails in America, going all the way from Georgia to Maine, most of it through woods and uninhabited land. Everyone should get away from civilization occasionally."

He waited for a response. I looked at him with wide eyes, taking in the impossibility of walking from Georgia to Maine.

"Sure, we'll check it out," I said.

He nodded. "If you continue up this hill, you can get right on it. Well, be safe out there. You two seem like lovely girls. I hope you find good husbands."

I rolled my eyes. Not this flaming homosexual. But in spite of his assumptions about me, something in me clicked.

I looked up the trail's stats on my phone. The thought of hiking a 2,193-mile trail across fourteen states was inconceivable. I had only ever hiked casually, taking day trips, but even those were rare. Now this forest was calling out to me. It was a whisper, a nudge, a spiritual invitation to the wild. Something invisible and unforeseen drew me to the trail. Something as mystical as the dragonflies that had always seemed to follow me since I was a child. At this point, unemployed and mentally dehydrated, my mind needed to be saturated, my thirst needed to be quenched. And just like that, the Appalachian Trail had me mesmerized.

When I got home, I went on Facebook to search for hiking groups geared toward the Appalachian Trail. I wanted to see if others had attempted such an intense feat. My effort yielded hundreds of results. I clicked JOIN and was added to New Jersey hiking and Appalachian Trail groups, with communities of twenty thousand to sixty thousand followers. Each day, I watched countless YouTube videos. I was getting sucked in, until there was no turning back.

I was going to hike the Appalachian Trail.

Inevitably, barriers soon presented themselves. How would I get gear? How could I afford this? What about my safety as a Black woman, especially in the South? Just weeks before my decision to hike the AT, on February 23, 2020, Ahmaud Arbery, a Black man, was shot while jogging by two racist white men in south Georgia, and the news had sickened me. From its starting point in Georgia, the Appalachian Trail proceeded through red states like Tennessee, Pennsylvania, and West Virginia.

Frightened, I did some research online. Seeing nothing on the topic of racism on the trail, I typed a question in one of the Facebook groups: *Should I be concerned as a Black woman hiking in the South?* The keyboard seemed so far away, and each letter felt like the keystroke that might ignite a bomb as I typed. My question posted, I went to bed.

The next morning, I opened my laptop to scan the page, a detective looking for clues. Instead, I found a crime scene, and *I* was being interrogated.

What does racism have to do with hiking?

The trees don't see color.

The root cause of racism is poverty.

Black people don't hike because most Black kids don't have a father.

Don't bring politics into this group.

Stop being a race baiter.

You aren't special.

You aren't the first Black person to hike the AT.

My stomach sank. Each comment rattled me.

And then something happened. I felt like I finally understood why I was often surrounded by dragonflies. I had been a nymph, having spent years beneath the surface, feeding on tadpoles, nearly comatose. But with this jolt, this challenge from people who couldn't see me or understand me, I was ready to emerge. First came my membranous wings, and then emerged my mouth, ready to speak truths that no one wanted to hear. I shed my skin even though it left me vulnerable to the predators of social media.

I started to write.

I took a hammer to the keyboard, pounding each letter, willing myself to be heard. My emotions poured into the blank white canvas of the screen, and my words reached the ears of members in the Facebook group first, then college professors, hiking gear companies, and strangers who all gathered in support of me as I brought light to the stories and inequities disproportionately affecting BIPOC hikers and shared my plan to thru-hike the Appalachian Trail. My wingspan reached wide, spreading awareness. Advocating for the voices of the unheard in the hiking community became my calling.

One day, my phone rang as a streak of sunlight came through my broken white shutters. *Who is calling me at the crack of dawn?* The words HARPERS FERRY appeared on the screen. I hit the green button.

"Hello?"

"Hello, is this Shilletha? My name is Safwan. I heard about what happened to you on that Facebook group."

I woke up fully.

"Really?"

"Yes. The article you wrote in response really touched my heart. I am a Middle Eastern man who thru-hiked the AT around 9/11, and I endured all sorts of racism. No one wants to talk about it, but we get reports all the time."

"It was strange to get so much resistance," I said. "But somehow it just makes me want to go even more."

"Believe me, I know that feeling. I know you plan to thru-hike next year, and I spoke to the Appalachian Trail Conservancy on your behalf. We are interested in sponsoring you."

In his voice, a furnace burned that matched mine. My truth came to life. I could not extinguish his pain, but I could validate it. And I could share it. We had walked this path together even though our stories differed.

My gears began to shift, and the universe suddenly changed its course, sweeping me along in its wake. It took no effort at all, like the wind catching a baby bird attempting to fly. The first leap from the tree for any fledgling is always the most jarring, but with faith, I knew my wings would carry me, the same wings that over the course of my life had been clipped, broken, and shredded.

I knew faith would have to get me from Georgia to Maine because that was all I had. I knew the journey forward would be hard because the past threatened to catch up with each step I took. I knew I would be beaten down again and again—physically, emotionally, spiritually. But I also knew that I had to keep walking; if not, I would sink.

SPRINGER MOUNTAIN, GEORGIA

In February of 2021, I found myself standing at the trailhead of Springer Mountain in Georgia, my heart quaking in my chest. The sun did not care to shine her light that winter day, and so I accepted her bargain—maybe later she would embrace me and soothe my unrelenting nerves. Waiting was what I knew; anything good in life was worth waiting for. And thus I found myself here, ten months after I received the good news from Safwan that the Appalachian Trail Conservatory would sponsor my thru-hike, in front of a bronze plaque embedded in a boulder that marked the southern terminus of the Appalachian Trail. A map of fourteen states, stretching from

Georgia to Maine, was ingrained in gold, with a bold line running through the heart of them.

SPRINGER MOUNTAIN, ELEVATION 3,782, it read, adjacent to the elaborate artwork. To the right of the boulder stood a trail register. I pulled the handle of its drawer and found my first hiker log. It was nothing special, just your typical composition book, the kind you doodled in back in grade school, and placed in a gallon Ziploc bag to shelter it from the elements. This notebook symbolized the start of a new cycle. I was still relatively fresh to hiker culture, and I reveled in the simplicity of the way we communicated through pen and paper. Phone service wasn't guaranteed anyway, so I figured I'd make my mark to officially begin my new odyssey the good old-fashioned way.

Dragonsky was here. I wrote my trail name in cursive.

I told myself I wouldn't sign the registers too often. Safety was key, and I didn't know what could happen, but I did know that there had been thirteen murders from 1974 to 2019 on the AT, and not everyone was a fan of my work.

Over the past few months, I had become "hiker famous" from my 2020 article that had gone viral, and people knew what I had come to do from the reels I posted of myself preparing for the AT. Social media could find me out here in the woods, where my identity could not be concealed. I was the only Black woman with locs that I knew of on the trail.

My trail name, Dragonsky, was birthed half a year previously on the steeple ledge of a mountain on the Suffern–Bear Mountain Trail in the summer of 2020 while I was training for the AT. I had agreed to hike with Alex, a man I barely knew, for two days. His demeanor was overbearing and passive-aggressive, and I was keeling over from a combination of psychedelic mushrooms and perilous period cramps.

"You're not going fast enough!"

"I'm doing my best," I snapped.

I barreled down the trail until I flew off it and slammed my shin into a boulder. Blood gushed down my leg. The wound was not my immediate priority; it was concealing my pain and tears, which was useless—they streamed down my face, and our eyes met.

"What's wrong? Why are you crying?"

"You told me I wasn't going fast enough, and I tried but fell into this boulder. Fuck! I can't lead. It makes me anxious!" I said.

"I don't have time for your emotions. You need to go find someone to deal with that," he said.

I walked a few hundred feet off trail into an open space in the woods to find a quiet spot to calm myself. I climbed a smooth oval-shaped boulder without grooves for my feet. I fell on the first attempt, my pack acting as a pillow, taking the impact of my fall. I attempted it a second time, with success. I perched myself up on the flat top, sitting cross-legged, crying with my head buried in my hands.

What an idiot I am! Coming out here with a strange man, in this gloomy weather, and not knowing how to survive.

Sulking, feeling completely absorbed in my sorrows, I barely noticed that something had landed on my head. The buzzing of its wings beat loudly in my ears. Baffled, I put my hands on the crown of my head to touch the unknown object and felt its soft wings. Startled, it flew to my shoe and stayed perfectly still like a statue. It was an orange dragonfly. Delicate yet robust, she twirled in the air and then landed back on my shoe. She stayed by my side until my tears ceased, her energy relaying to me that I was not alone. In fact, I was never alone. The dragonflies always came to me when I needed them. Smiling, I looked up and saw the gray sky crack open as the light of the sun shone down on me.

"Dragonsky," I said. "That's my name. I am Dragonsky."

A trail name, part of thru-hiking culture, is usually given by others based on one's appearance, mishaps, personality, or activities. It is the gifting of a new identity and the shedding of the old one, an act of being reborn. The trail is a place to be free of labels, including ones bestowed by our parents. Government names are typically not spoken: No one wants to know who you were; they want to know who you are. Freedom and liberation are taken seriously on trail, and when you find yourself, you become new—like a dragonfly emerging from the water. For me, Dragonsky was a warrior and a fighter, a fierce predator, powerful yet delicate, birthed from nature and created into a new being. When Dragonsky saw fear, she ran toward it. There was nothing she couldn't do, and she would find her freedom in the wilderness. She—I—never looked back.

I put the hiking logbook back into its drawer. I stood tall and buckled my two ivory-black chest harness straps and pulled each side of my hip belt taut. The belt nestled itself right on the saddle of my hips and adhered nicely to my body. My scrawny legs nearly buckled as I adjusted my blue pack and felt its weight on my back.

Sunrise to sunset, I would be carrying twenty-six pounds that consisted of my shelter, sleep system, cook pot, food, three sets of clothes, a down puffy coat, rain gear, a water filter and bladder, an umbrella, and common sense. Anything but the bare necessities was a luxury item, a waste of weight, or, worse, a strain on the body. The goal, always, was to leave behind as much as possible.

But even with few material items, I took my first steps on the Appalachian Trail with the weight of the world on my back. At least I had Donna by my side. Donna was a "Dragonfly," a nickname I gave my supporters and fans, many of whom had offered to be my trail angels to help me along the trail whenever I needed. Donna was one of them. She had picked me up from the airport in Atlanta, graciously opened her home to me, fed me generously, and offered to walk with me to touch my first white blaze—the famous route markers of the AT—before we said goodbye. Days ago we had been cyber friends, and now here we were in the flesh, taking on nature's fury together.

Donna was a veteran and a mom of two who lived in the presence of the mountains in north Georgia. She stood like a telephone pole, never swaying in the wind. Each step she took had poise and grace, and I could tell her soul was pure and full of love. We spoke about her time in the military, her community, and tips for the trail as we walked. Teaching excited her.

"You know, there are three uses for your trowel." She gestured to the aluminum sky-blue trowel dubbed the Deuce. "You can use it as a splint for if you injure or break your wrist—just wrap some KT Tape around it to add support. That's one."

I nodded.

"Number two, you obviously use it to dig and bury poop. And number three, you can use it as a weapon."

My eyes widened. *Tell me more.*

"Just get some paracord or something strong, loop it through that little hole at the bottom of the trowel, and sleep with that on your wrist. If someone messes with you, you stab 'em!"

I was in awe, desperate to learn more tips on how to fend for myself and be self-sufficient. I knew some female hikers went out on the trail knowing they could ask male hikers to help set up their gear for them, but being a damsel in distress was not what I wanted. I wanted to go out independently, trusting my gear and my own knowledge of how to utilize and repair it. I wanted any future success to be mine, and mine alone.

I admired Donna's fearlessness. She taught me what she had learned in the military. I couldn't show fear in this jungle, she said, because if I acted like prey, then I was prey. She didn't falter, and so neither did I.

Our time spent together was meaningful and short. I had never known such kindness from a stranger, and when it came time to depart my eyes welled with tears, but I knew I had to do the trail alone. After we bid each other farewell, I glanced back. She was gone. I was now alone in the woods of the Chattahoochee National Forest.

The gravity of the moment struck me. I was hiking the AT, solo. I was finally doing what I had set out to do, what I had told the world I would do in spite of naysayers' best intentions to discourage me.

In my commitment to doing so, I was leaving behind my friends and my dog, Meraxes, in the matrix of civilization while I set out to conquer the world.

I clasped my hands and closed my eyes, feeling the light touch my skin. In that moment, it felt like a dragonfly had just landed on me, like the one that had done so many months ago. Her wings were as long as her delicate body, shimmering in the colors of the softest rainbow. She was radiant. Sensing my doubts, fears, and insecurities, she gathered me to her bosom and sprinkled me with her miracle dust. With her divine intervention, I knew I was ready to push on. I was ready to break the chains of trauma and find liberation in my truth.

WANING CRESCENT

Before I was destined for the white blazes, before I found my voice in the hiking community, I was a little girl in New Jersey maneuvering the earth with the magic of her wings.

Fun-sized, they called me, which was accurate. Shoulders were platforms to sit on, and countertops were mountains to climb. Cavernous depths lay under the bed. There was rarely a place I couldn't fit in or get to. Chocolate from my Nigerian, Congolese, Cameroonian, and Ghanaian roots covered every inch of my skin, leaving an even pigment and texture, soft as a puppy's belly. Three braided ponytails secured ballies that hung off the roots of my permed African kinky hair, complete with a surplus of flimsy, colorful plastic barrettes clipped on at the ponytail tips. Coke-bottle glasses sat on my wide, stubby nose. Nothing was able to puncture the glass except for the soccer ball a friend and I kicked around the patch of weathered grass by the church. That soccer ball claimed three pairs.

I spent most of my time with my great-aunt Barbara and great-uncle Amos. Their humble abode was a cozy white three-bedroom ranch-style home with maroon shutters in Manchester, a small town in South Jersey, or "SoJ." Manchester was in an ideal location, only eleven miles from Seaside Heights beach and pier, thirty minutes from Six Flags Great Adventure, and about two hours from what we called "the City," known to others as New York City. The home came complete with a favorable amount of land, all well-kept, thanks to my uncle. The backyard became my oasis and escape; we had an in-ground Jacuzzi, a swing set, and eventually a trampoline that I was gifted after working hard in school and receiving good grades on my report card. I was always fed savory home-cooked meals that I indulged in until my stomach was way past full. Living with my aunt and uncle was the picture of the American dream: a typical heterosexual married couple in their mid-fifties with two cars—even if one was a lemon, a *smoking* lemon. We had it all: a half-rotted white picket fence, a few dogs, and neighbors whose kind demeanors always seemed too good to be true.

This comparative luxury was my second home in the mix of the three that I rotated through frequently—between my aunt and uncle, my grandmother whom I called Momma Nan, and my biological mother.

Whether a life of love, comfort, and safety was laid out in the cards for me was questionable from birth. As a fetus tucked within the comfort of my mother's womb, my destiny was precarious. While my mother maintains she was not addicted to drugs with me, my family members have told me that I had many of the symptoms of babies born addicted to crack.

As I grew up, stability was scarce. I bounced from riches in Manchester with my aunt to a small two-bedroom apartment with my mother and grandmother in Morristown. Poverty was a cycle, and being a child in poverty was a whirlwind. The United States has the second-highest child poverty rate among the world's developed countries—and I was a part of that statistic. We weren't drastically poor, but in comparison to Aunt Barbara's abundance, soup kitchens and church missions were where my grandmother took us to eat hot meals and pick up clothes that we did not have the ability or privilege to buy. Ketchup sandwiches, Oodles of Noodles, and loaves of bread that I rolled into balls filled my belly with starches and carbohydrates. And so, between my mother, my grandmother in Morristown and my aunt and uncle, I was glad to have at least one place where I truly felt at home.

Aunt Barbara had married into the family via my maternal grandmother's brother. She was a deeply religious Black woman. An evangelist and teacher in the church, she was well respected. Gardening and cooking soul-warming Southern baked macaroni and cheese were her specialties. Her mocha skin and few wrinkles gave no hint of the rugged childhood she had endured in North Carolina with her two siblings, or of her own raising of two beautiful girls, my cousins. Painting was one of her hidden talents, and nearly every morning she pulled out her paints and oils and created a masterpiece on her face. Dusting her soft cheeks with pink blush, she swept back and forth with a light stroke of the brush. Various hues of blue, purple, and red emerged on her eyelids. Her plump lips stood out boldly in dark red. She spoke with the light words of an angel and sang with a voice that moved mountains.

Uncle Amos had dark-chocolate skin and stood about five foot seven. Sea salt was a familiar scent that lingered on him, as he worked countless hours at Morton Salt, driving a dump truck out to the endless salt pyramids on the land. Uncle Amos was good at his job and took pride in his work, so much so that he would bring salt crystals home for me to admire. For a man in his late fifties, he was very fit, and he would often take long walks throughout our quaint suburban neighborhood. In Uncle Amos's day, working in the field picking cotton and getting reprimanded by your neighbors was a way of life. Segregation was an era he had lived though. Families with eight or more children were the norm, and his consisted of twelve. He was also deeply religious, and a deacon and minister in the church. He always looked his Sunday best in his nice black suits. Sunday mornings, I would stand right beside him as he handed out the church brochures and greeted those who came in. I wanted to be like him.

I was always encouraged by my aunt and uncle to learn and explore. I took advantage of the privilege and constantly played outside. I was a natural-born earth child. Roly-polies, lighting bugs, and cactus needles found themselves at home with me, an excellent host. I admired nature and respected the other souls and creatures who shared this earth. Discovery Channel and Animal Planet were my go-to programs on TV, as I was fascinated by animals, especially the cheetah. Some mornings when the wind was still, I was able to smell the tranquil, salty air of the majestic Atlantic Ocean just a few miles away. At the beach, I loved to collect the seashells that washed up on the shore and draw circles and shapes into the wet sand with sticks I'd found by the dunes. I admired the waves as they crashed with power against the shoreline, only to retreat. I knew the ocean could be as calm as a hibernating bear one day, and the next execute destruction upon the land with hurricanes, floods, and tsunamis. I also found it fascinating how the moon, sun, and ocean worked in sync with each other to form waves, cyclical patterns that repeated again and again.

I was in the sixth grade in the summer of 2002. The air was thick with humidity. There I was, in Aunt Barbara's bedroom, sitting on her comfortable gray carpet, crisscross applesauce, my dark brown eyes large and my body leaning forward in anticipation of the news. Aunt Barbara sat upon the flower-print comforter on her queen-sized bed while the thirty-second timer song from *Jeopardy* filled the silence. She grabbed the remote, pressed the red OFF button.

"We are going to go to Florida for vacation, and we will be staying in the Palms resort."

"Where in Florida?"

"Kissimmee."

Mwah! I planted a huge kiss on my aunt's left cheek.

Aunt Barbara let out a slight giggle, which turned into a full-blown laugh. I looked at my aunt in confusion.

"Kissimmee is the name of the town our resort is in, but we will be going to Orlando, and—"

Before she could finish her sentence, my mind went to that magical place that nearly every kid dreamed about.

"DISNEY WORLD? WHEN?!"

"A few weeks from now."

It would be my first big vacation. I counted down the weeks until we would depart. Patience was not a virtue of mine, and I asked every day when we were going. Thankfully, the weeks flew by, as I passed them by watching *Dragon Ball Z* and whatever else was on Cartoon Network, until we left one day at about four in the morning. The thought was that if I stayed up all night, I would sleep through the whole car ride and wake up at our destination. When the time came, I was already dressed in my car clothes, had my suitcase packed, and had prepared my car kit that consisted of nonrestrictive purple sweatpants and a sweatshirt that I would wear for the next twenty-three hours. I also had my blue teddy bear Nevaeh, my red Game Boy Advance SP, and my blue blanket. I grabbed my suitcase and climbed confidently into the back seat of our silver rental car. I was so excited about rental cars, as they usually had that new car smell and advanced things like butt heaters. I lay in the back seat, cuddled Nevaeh, wrapped myself in my blanket, closed my eyes, and drifted away, exhausted. Hours later, I woke up and looked out of the passenger window to see miles of lush grass and trees. We were in North Carolina.

It was a familiar drive, as we traveled down Interstate 95 at least twice a year to North Carolina to visit most of our family. I was not amused in the least; we were in what I considered to be the most boring place in the world. I vanished back into the world of sleep and eventually woke up around eight. Stars danced in the night sky, but there was no trace of the moon. I always looked for the moon. She was my guiding force.

Sixteen hours and nine minutes passed rather swiftly, and finally, elegant palm trees of all sizes lined the highway.

"Mama, wake up!" Aunt Barbara said in a thunderous voice. *Mama* was the name my aunt called me. She would say, "Mama, are you winning?" I would respond with a headshake yes, and she would yell, "You go, girl!" It was our little thing.

I jumped up because I knew we had reached our destination. I was blind as a bat without my glasses, so I had to squint.

Bold white font appeared on the midnight-blue canvas: WELCOME TO FLORIDA, THE SUNSHINE STATE. The *O* was an image of the sun.

Orlando, Florida, became the symbol and icon of what dreams lay ahead of me. Disney World gave me hope and opened my mind to possibilities I couldn't even fathom as a sheltered eleven-year-old girl. I visited Epcot, Magic Kingdom, and my favorite park of all, Animal Kingdom. The day I went to Animal Kingdom, the sun welcomed me and kissed my brown cheeks. The sky was a baby-blue canvas painted with calm white cirrus clouds. The temperature was tropical—perfect for a thin little girl with anemia. I walked around with my uncle while my aunt stayed back at the resort, as she wasn't feeling too well. Everywhere we walked, there were habitats for creatures of every kind—amphibians, birds, and primates, just to name a few. I found my niche among the arthropods. As I walked through the park's enchanting forest, I was drawn to a ranger holding an insect in her hand. My curiosity got the better of me, and I picked up my pace and headed over to the ranger. In her hand was a brilliant royal-blue exoskeleton, four translucent wings, and two huge black eyes that nearly took up all the space on the head of a three-inch insect.

"What is that?" I asked the ranger.

"This is the dragonfly. They come in many colors, and they are very curious about us." She continued, "Dragonflies have big mouths, but they only bite when threatened. They don't sting, they love to eat mosquitoes, and they hover around us in curiosity. They don't mean any harm."

My mouth was agape, and I was in awe of the information I had just obtained. I was an instant fan.

"Would you like to touch the dragonfly?" she asked.

"YES!" I eagerly reached out and stroked the back of the dragonfly. Her skin was hard like a wooden stick, and I made sure not to touch her delicate wings. *Dragonfly.* This core memory and fascination would stay with me.

I didn't know it then, but in almost every culture of the world, the dragonfly symbolizes maturity—both mental and emotional—depth of character, power, and poise. These creatures can move at an unbelievable forty-five miles per hour in all directions, yet they can abruptly stop to hover, like a hummingbird. I adopted the dragonfly as my muse, and she became a symbol of strength, perseverance, and adventure for me, as well as of balance and change.

That day at Animal Kingdom, I also learned about veterinarians. At the time, I knew them simply as "animal doctors." In front of the African lion habitat, one of the park's veterinarians spoke to a group of onlookers about what it took to become a vet: a tedious career path, requiring at least eight years of advanced schooling, compassion, great attention to detail, hands-on practice, and a lot of hardcore math and science classes like calculus and organic chemistry. In my young, naive mind, I had no concept of what college really was or how much hard work it would be. Nor was I aware that college was a privilege rather than a right, and that not everyone had the means to pursue higher education. I was simply a young girl with ambition and aspirations of becoming a veter-inarian. I discovered I had a connection with animals and a deep passion for nursing them back to health. I was so determined to be a vet that when I got back home, I created a mock degree on a piece of tan construction paper and wrote my name, substituting my aunt's last name because I so badly wanted to belong to her family, and *Doctor of Veterinary Medicine*. I decorated the outside of the "degree" with a zigzag border in blue marker created with the help of my wooden ruler, and lastly, I sealed my work of art with my signature in amateurish cursive.

On our last day, we went to Sea World. The park transported me into a world of massive coral reefs and underwater sea caves, giving me a window into a mysterious environment where humans would never be able to survive. We saw penguins, polar bears, orcas, and—my favorite—dolphins. Mammals with keen intelligence and rubbery skin, dolphins intrigued me. As I waited in line, a small opening appeared between a group of people. I took that opportunity to squeeze in and noticed a dolphin right in front of me. Once again, adrenaline ran through my tiny body. She was upright in the water with her fins apart and what looked like a smile on her face. Her skin was a smooth metallic gray. She had a long snout, perfect medium-black circular eyes, and a small dorsal fin on her lean figure. The trainer had her lie on her stomach and put her head down so we could pet her without falling into the water. I didn't yet know how to swim, and the thought of drowning lingered in the back of my mind.

I decided at that moment to be brave. I took a deep breath and reached out. My tiny brown hand made contact with the dolphin's back, and then her side. I was totally immersed and present in that moment. Our eyes connected, mammal to mammal, no judgment and no concerns. It was as if I were one with the dolphin. Her intelligence was indescribable. Her body felt like smooth, slippery butter, shiny and new. There were no dings or scratches on her, nor me; we were both in our youth. It did not matter that I walked upright on two legs while she swam with ease using her powerful fins. We were born of the same earth, and we would return to the earth in due time.

When the time came to say goodbye to Sea World, the last stop on the way out was the gift shop, following standard amusement attraction protocol, and I was given permission to pick one memento. I walked around the boring stuff like logoed shirts and baseball caps. I had nearly given up my quest when a shiny object caught my eye. I turned around as my gaze came to rest on a beautiful snow globe. There were orcas within, and the base was outlined in waves and sea grass. I knew I had to have it.

I power walked over to the small shelf, picked up the fragile knickknack, and handed it to my uncle. "I want this globe!"

It was nearly twenty-five dollars, which was a lot to me. It would have taken me more than two months to acquire such loot, as my allowance was five dollars every other week. Uncle Amos gave in and spoiled me with the snow-globe splurge. His generosity was not wasted, for that globe still sits in my room to this very day.

Every time I look at the snow globe, it transports me back to the good old days. The days when I felt safe, protected, free, and open. Little did I know that I was on a beautiful, but fictional, path that I produced in my mind. I imagined that life would always be like the new moon. During a new moon, the earth, sun, and moon align, just as they do in a full moon. This new moon in Florida represented a new beginning, a blank slate, an open heart, and a naive trust. I had no idea that when we returned to New Jersey, my utopia would slowly vanish.

My life was going to be a fight. It would take me years to find my place and purpose. To be the woman my aunt raised. I would suffer. I would plead. I would long to reconcile the sins of my past. I would want relief from the mental illnesses that began to infiltrate my life, following me like an angry hornet, stinging without rhyme or reason. Leaving me out in the cold and waiting to die.

3

BIG BUTT BYPASS, TENNESSEE

Depression is like being trapped in a treacherous blizzard in the mountain wilderness. It feels like a soulless being slipping a dark cloak over my face, kidnapping me and dropping me off in the remote arctic where the landscape is void of trails and roads, where civilization has not left its imprint. It is like being on a mountain that has transcended the atmosphere and created its own realm, where a blizzard presses her weight upon the dense alpine forest as the temperatures drop below freezing. I either navigate my way through the blizzard in vain, lost and blinded by the fog, or I simply strip and die from exposure.

It was during mile 298 of the Appalachian Trail, Big Butt Bypass in eastern Tennessee, when the trail presented me with that opportunity to die. I had come to a split in the trail that gave me two options: the white blaze that said EXPOSED RIDGELINE TRAIL or the blue blaze for the BAD WEATHER TRAIL. Had I been a purist, the choice would have been simple—the white blaze, no matter what. That was the true AT, according to some thru-hikers. But conditions were not favorable; it was foggy, and precipitation crept in. The high route was noted to be a rocky scramble, where I'd need to navigate roots and crawl up boulders. The scramble rewarded thru-hikers with magnificent views, which I would miss anyway because of the weather. Nature and I were in the same mood, and the choice was made for me by a rumble in the distance. I followed my instinct and stayed low on the trail meant for bad weather.

Next up was Big Butt Bypass. It seemed humorous at the time when I checked my map. Why would anyone name it that? But on the Appalachian Trail, nothing made sense. There were places named Chunky Gal Trail, Swag of the Blue Ridge, and my personal favorite, Highcock Knob, whose summit featured artwork ingrained into a rock deemed the Tip of Highcock. After what felt like climbing the StairMaster 5000 every day since I had started on the trail, a good laugh was as welcome as a cold beer. My goal was to get to the site and pull out my phone for a selfie of my butt near the sign.

I had left Georgia some time back, and it was starting to sink in that I was actually on the AT, thru-hiking. But I was forging a new belief that the AT might become the biggest mistake of my life. Had I acted too soon? I had set out to hike the trail to change the narrative around being Black outdoors, to inspire others, and, most importantly, to find myself. The puzzle of my life was made up of missing pieces, and I wanted to piece them together again. I needed to complete the picture. But the truth was, at least two states in, I was consumed with my depression and suicidal thoughts. Since I'd begun hiking, suicidal and negative thoughts seldom crossed my mind, but whenever they did, it was all or nothing.

Why was I out here? Was I worthy of my dog, Meraxes, whom I had left behind with my cousin in North Carolina? Was I worthy of any good thing at all?

Another question was taking root in my mind, even though I had set out to thru-hike solo. Would I ever find a tramily on the AT? A tramily is one of the highlights of the trail, where others hike with you 24/7/365, forming an irreplaceable bond that might otherwise take years to forge in the unnatural world. I saw it with my own eyes: hikers taking care of each other, camping together, and even yellow-blazing—skipping sections of trail—just to keep up with their newfound family. It is a family unlike any other, one that understands the triumphs and yearnings of the wild, as well as the stench that goes along with the turmoil of thru-hiking the AT. *Family* was a word that had dissipated into thin air when I was younger, and now I was eager to find it, a new chosen family to push me on to Katahdin in Maine, the ending point of the AT.

Nobody believed I would make it to Maine anyway; it was a statement I'd heard over and over from a few people close to me. The truth was I knew I *could* make it, at least if depression didn't beat me to Katahdin. Every morning, I woke up to the sun and a bottle of antidepressants—Wellbutrin and Remeron—to give me the will to live. I took my medication religiously, taking my Wellbutrin in the mornings, as it provided energy, and Remeron in the evenings, as it put me to sleep. I decided not to take Adderall on my hike lest I suddenly drop dead from too much strain on my heart. I've always wanted to die in nature—but not by drugs. After my Wellbutrin, I usually broke down camp, ate a quick meal of instant oatmeal, and took fifteen minutes to stretch before heading out.

On the morning of my hike to Big Butt Bypass, I skipped this morning routine. Instead, I found myself weeping, and not just because I was cold and my tent zippers had frozen over; it was because my soul ached. I had no friends to reach out to, and I wanted to die. As I walked, I cried. I paused for a moment, clinging to the moist wall of boulders on my right, inching over the edge. I saw a light in the darkness, an escape from my sorrows down a steep embankment. I thought of how defective I was, having to remind myself through my chemical needs that there was something wrong with me.

I stared at my arms for several moments, and a series of horrible images washed over me. Horrible, horrible images. I could see hundreds of cuts, the wounds as white as fish, my skin dangling from my body. My scarlet blood, racing down my arms to an invisible finish line. Oh, how I yearned for a razor. It was nicotine. It made me feel good while slowly killing me. The satisfaction it brought was addictive, because I was nothing. I was a fallen leaf. A droplet of water in the lake. Nothing.

Please, I can't bear this darkness again. Please don't come back . . . please . . . I'm begging you. Don't leave me out here, isolated in the wilderness, to die from this.

Consumed by existential guilt, I sank into another version of myself. The version I had tried so hard to fix in the past fourteen years of therapy, with endless orange bottles of antidepressants and mood stabilizers, inpatient hospitalizations, and now hiking. Nature was a healer, but she could not cure me. She could not take away the endless nights of crying myself to sleep or stop me from splitting my wrists wide open. Yes, she comforted me and removed me from the distractions of our fictional world, releasing me back into the wild. Out here, there was no judgment or fear that my ADHD or depression would ruin my job or that people were judging me. I could be myself, and that was freeing. But it wasn't enough. It didn't help that I had stopped therapy when I started the trail, simply because the unpredictable nature of the terrain, climate, socializing, and occasional trail magic always interfered with my schedule. Plus, cell service was a privilege. Simply put, I hadn't prioritized it, and now I was paying the price.

I pulled out my GoPro to record a video of my last words. There was nothing to look forward to except the oven they would burn my body in.

"Hey everyone, this is Dragonsky. I am not having a good day on trail—in fact, I hate myself. I am a piece of shit who belongs under someone's shoe. Every day, I struggle with depression, and today it won. I am so tired of suffering and battling my worthless thoughts. I have no will to live. Why should I? I was a fool for coming out here with severe recurrent depression, thinking that I could cope and be fine with meds. Well, I'm not! I hate myself, life is pointless, and this will never get better for me. My depression keeps coming back and will forever be a part of my life. I can't take this anymore, I'm sorry . . . I need to die. This would be the best for everyone. I am not an inspiration. I am a burden, and I don't want to burden anyone anymore. I am defective. It doesn't fucking matter. NOTHING FUCKING MATTERS! FUCKING TIRED OF THIS SHIT!" I turned my camera off.

I was empty. I could not console myself. But even as I prepared for the end, standing there on the edge of the mountain and looking down to my death, I felt nothing yet *something*. I was nothing to these mountains, but they were everything to me.

The most prominent revelation to me was that here, there was no beating the trail. No magic tricks or magicians. No scheming or bargaining with the mountain. It was so very simple and blunt. There were only two options: I could go back in the direction I had come from, or I could move forward, confront obstacles, and face the shadows before me.

So many bystanders had told me I couldn't do it. But I had made a pact to complete the trail from the beginning to the end. Quitting was not an option. That was my commitment, and mental illness was not going to deter me.

After half an hour, I decided that I didn't want to die. Not now, not here. I looked north and took the only option I had. To keep walking. To keep fighting. I took a deep breath and wiped my tears away. I would live today.

Long before I had set out for the Appalachian Trail, I already knew the many situations in which my mental illness might bloom while out here: the absolute darkness of the night, not having friends on trail, when exhaustion had me thinking about dying on steep mountain climbs, the thought of being killed by a dangerous man, the sounds of the wild. I knew that if I gave in to my fears, my hike would come to a sorrowful end. Like all warriors, I had a safety plan in case of a crisis when my medication and coping skills were not adequate. My first step was to call a friend, but as I currently had no bars on my phone, that was quickly abandoned. Step two was to smoke weed.

Weed was the center and joy of my life. It was neither a crutch nor an addiction but rather a healer and a reliever of chronic pain. I studied it meticulously like the codings of a computer, learning how the plethora of strains and their medicinal uses affected the body. In one puff of herb, my mood lifted. As nature's Xanax took charge, my mind transcended the realm of time and space. My mind focused on the mysteries of the universe. *What are black holes? How come there is foam in the water? Whoa! What type of bird is that?* Marijuana allowed ideas to flourish, bringing out deep curiosities like those of a young child while crushing the demons that lurked. I walked down the trail and talked to myself. I was shocked by my new affirmations.

This is meant to be. I'm going to make it to Katahdin. I know who I am. I am Dragonsky.

Growing up, I had sworn off drugs, claiming that I would never open that Pandora's box of addiction. But I'd been smoking weed for years to help stimulate the appetite that Adderall suppressed, and it had gotten me through panic attacks and period cramps, celebrations and losses. Thankfully, smoking is at the core of trail culture. *Safety meetings* on the trail is the code word for *Let's get high*. It's a celebration for surviving hours ascending and descending mountains that make our kneecaps slide like old records being rubbed together. When class was in session, a host would present their safety items—a bowl, rolling papers, grinder, lighter, and our esteemed guest: Mary Jane. The host packed the bowl or blunt and passed it around the group for inhalable goodness. Smoking was a way of bonding, winding down for the day, and making instant mashed potatoes taste like a loaded twice-baked masterpiece smothered in gooey cheddar.

Weed handed me a rope to pull me back onto the Bypass, but I knew depression never struck just once. I knew that my depression would grow like the stem of a greenbrier, its spiny thorns weaving upward toward the sky, climbing and conquering any life beneath it. I also knew the power of asking for what I wanted, that faith and manifestation were in my hands. *Ask and you shall receive*. No matter what, the trail would provide. And provide it did.

Tonic was a legend, and everyone knew of him. He was known for his specialty drug collection, with reviews raving about the quality and affordability of his products. The night after I bargained with nature, our paths crossed at a hostel in Erwin, Tennessee. I sat next to him under a river of stars by the roaring campfire, smoking a blunt, talking about the lack of Black people on trail.

"You ever try acid?" He'd been dropping it twice a week and had a steady influx of customers. "It helps with my depression, bro. Like, I am able to get out of my head and shit. I love taking it on trail, that shit makes you do miles with good vibes. You should try it on trail. How much you wanna buy? I'll throw you one for free."

His entire being—the way he chuckled, the grit in his eyes, his surfer voice and those "bros" and "yeah, dudes"—was pure and charming, a way of being I never believed I could achieve. Getting out of my head seemed impossible, but with acid, maybe I could have a day of normality. I ached to be that way: free from depression, flowing through the trail like a river, becoming one with the mountain.

I couldn't resist. At five dollars a pop, I bought five tabs and slipped them into a plastic sandwich bag. The next morning we said our goodbyes, and I went for gold. I pulled out a tab the size of a kernel of corn and placed it under my tongue for ten minutes, absorbing the fullness of the substance. This wasn't just for fun. I was not going to be an addict. I was willing to try it for the sake of my life; that was the reality of it. The antidepressants worked, and then they failed. They gave me happiness, then left me sobbing in the wilderness. But acid worked.

I packed up, left the hostel, and continued on the trail, jamming to "Stubborn Love" by the Lumineers, moving my hips from side to side, spinning in circles with my trekking poles held high in the air like antennas. White auras started forming around the rhododendron and mountain laurel as if they were heavenly beings crowned in golden halos. My heart thudded as if I were raving at a concert; my hands trembled with excitement. Perception of myself went from *I'm a piece of shit* to *I am the shit!* I had no idea what I was doing as I walked, babbling to myself and touching my fingers to make sure they were still attached to my hands. I only knew that I had become the opposite of what I was. Someone fun. Someone free. Someone normal. I was finally awake, free of dread, embracing the trees, singing loudly.

And then the trail took a wide turn. Standing before me was a behemoth of a mountain, gaining two thousand feet in three miles. I lingered a little while, waiting for a sign to commemorate the start of my first climb on acid, but then I realized there were no bells or whistles; I just had to do it. So I did.

The trail was narrow and ran alongside the stream at the base, then dipped down a few feet before beginning a long climb in full exposure of the unrelenting sun. Within an hour I was flushed with sweat, the drugs warming me up, my calves dusted with the pale dirt that dominated the dry, rocky mountain face. *I'm okay*, I chanted repeatedly to myself, scared that I would die from heatstroke or a heart attack. I convinced myself that my words were true, that the panicked feeling was temporary, and that I would stop at the shelter in two miles. I knew if I allowed fear and panic to overcome me, my trip could turn deadly. I reasoned with myself, listening to folk music, guzzling water. I decided I was safe. I was brave. I could fight depression, despite the occasional thoughts of death. It took me two hours to find the shelter, and it felt like a dream, one that I wish I could have lived in forever.

I carried acid from that day forward with a heart of steel. But

even more important, I was walking on with a new truth: I could
stop my worthless thoughts. I could fight the cycle of depression.
I could climb mountains and talk myself off ledges. I did it once,
and I could do it again.

THIRD QUARTER MOON

Autumn came swiftly after our trip to Florida and blessed the land with crisp, cool air interrupted by bouts of heavy rain. Crimson, yellow, and green leaves danced and twirled in the wind. Homemade hot apple cider and freshly baked pumpkin pie seduced the senses, while the aroma of burning firewood eased the soul. Neon colors, boys in bomber jackets, and girls sporting tracksuits filled the Green in Morristown. *Rugrats*, *Out of the Box*, and *Looney Tunes* played on screens throughout the country. Bikes strewn about the front yard were a sign of the fun activities happening in the back. As adults we're nostalgic for the nineties because life was simple for us elementary school kids then.

Around that time, I had just landed back with my grandmother, Momma Nan, after another custody fight involving my aunt, uncle, and mother. This happened regularly throughout a large portion of my childhood, and when I landed back at my grandmother's, we were back at square one. I had a sister, Ayana, who was three years older than me. We hardly saw each other since we spent a lot of time in different homes, but this time our paths crossed. Ayana had lighter skin and delicate eyes. She was the more compliant and docile—and thus the more beloved—of the two of us. I, on the other hand, was the "wild child" who always got into mischief, at least to my grandmother.

Once, a few family members around my age and I went over to a friend's house, where a lavish meal of spaghetti with marinara sauce and crispy golden garlic bread was served. Due to my unstable upbringing, I had survivor syndrome, which meant I hoarded as much food as possible because I did not know when another meal would come, even if food was sufficient and plentiful. I inhaled my meal, barely coming up for air. Garlicky red marinara sauce clung to the corners of my mouth as I slurped down half a glass of refreshing cool water.

Later that night, some of my family members explained to me how embarrassed they were to have me at the table. Apparently, I had to pay for my lack of manners. They formed a circle around me and made me get into a squat position. Butt pushed out, knees bent, and arms at my side, I was scolded and beat with a belt if I moved from my position. I held back my tears, knowing I could not let them see that I was weak. I had done nothing wrong; I didn't deserve this humiliation. I knew they would never have treated my sister the way they treated me.

Perhaps if shaming couldn't "fix" me, getting rid of me altogether was an answer.

During the times when I wasn't with family, I hung out with Rhyme, my best friend since we were toddlers. Rhyme had what Black folks would call "good hair"—sleek, black, and easy to tame. Her curls did not curl as tightly as mine, so she didn't have to worry about her hair shrinking in the heat. Her eyes were honey, deep but also soft. Light-skinned, she had no issues with compliments and attention, while I on the other hand was considered dark and unattractive. Rhyme was so beautiful that I developed a crush on her, and we kissed once in fifth grade in her room. We spent every moment together, inseparable.

Our babysitter's house was two houses down from Rhyme's. I lived across town and had to walk about forty minutes to get there. The babysitter welcomed us with open arms and a loving home even though we slid down her stairs as if they were snowcapped mountaintops and used her porch chair pillows as walls for the forts we set up between gaps in the furniture. When we weren't inside, we were outside worm hunting and riding bikes down the hill into the painful bushes below.

On one particular day during the fall after the Disney trip, we made chicken-flavored Oodles of Noodles with an extra bouillon cube. After eating, I wanted to walk around the town, but Rhyme didn't. Being the independent child I was, I strolled off by myself and ended up at the Morristown train station. I was fascinated by trains and enjoyed looking at the cool older models. That day, I sat on the bench and watched as dozens of people walked down the stairs to the street or hurriedly ran to catch their already departing train. Classical music played through the speakers behind the loud sirens of the train horns.

In time, I decided it would be good to let Momma Nan know my whereabouts. I headed down to the pay phone to make a collect call. I don't remember if she answered or if I left a voicemail, but I do know my intended message was horribly misconstrued. I had simply stated, "I'm at the train station to look at trains. I'm going back to Rhyme's house now. Okay, bye."

To my grandmother, this had translated as me preparing to jump in front of a train. Later, I would be given a possible explanation as to how in the world she had come up with that interpretation, but at the time, I had no idea what caused her to think that. When I got back, Rhyme and I went digging for a worm to make our pet for the day, but we hadn't been in the street more than five minutes when the cops showed up.

Rhyme and I looked at each other. *What the hell is going on?* Little did I know that when the cop ushered me into his car, he would be taking me to the last place on earth that a young child should go—a psychiatric hospital.

As I lay between the thin white sheets of my hospital bed, anxiety hit me. How long would I be here?

"Please don't leave me here, Momma Nan. Please."

I knew no one was listening.

With no escape in sight, I knew the only way out was if Momma Nan agreed to sign me out, and if the psychiatrist deemed me safe enough to be discharged.

A peppy social worker in her early forties came into the room. She smiled genuinely.

"Shilletha?"

"Yes?" I replied.

"Can you tell me about what happened on the day you were brought here?"

I hesitated. I didn't know who this lady was, but I figured it couldn't hurt. I recounted the full story to her as I looked down at the hideous white floor.

"I am sorry that happened. It must have been frightening. Did you want to hurt yourself, Shilletha?"

My legs began to tremble as I felt a single drop of sweat run down my back.

"No."

I was bewildered. At about eleven years old, I had not yet experienced the urge to self-harm, nor the wrath of depression or anxiety. Regardless, it didn't matter what my story was. It didn't match up with whatever story Momma Nan had fabricated. I was a kid, and she was an adult. I didn't know if the social worker believed me or not. I knew I wasn't ill, but there I was, and there I was going to stay.

Hours after admission and paperwork, a staff member approached me. I was wearing a pink pair of Skechers with white laces that clashed with my purple two-piece sweat suit, which made me stand out like Barney the dinosaur.

"Strings, laces, and belts are not welcome here. They're a threat to your safety," said the staff member. My shoelaces were confiscated immediately.

Then I was led into a small private room by two nurses and subjected to a "body screen."

"Okay, honey, I am going to need you to get undressed. Take everything off, including your panties and socks. Ms. Elder and I have to conduct a scan of your body to look for any bruises, cuts, burns, or injuries. It's protocol that we do this for your safety and others'. We also want to make sure you get medical treatment if necessary."

"Um-m-m, o-o-o-kay . . ." I stammered.

I started gnawing away at my fingernails. I was reminded of my first roller coaster at Dollywood, the Tennessee Tornado. I hadn't been thrilled about going on this roller coaster, as it had loops, and the idea of being upside down was scary. But my cousin really wanted to go, and I was given no choice. Woefully, I crossed the metal air gates to get onto the train. Adrenaline surged through my body as our car climbed up the lift hill of the metal coaster. Every click reminded me that we were one step closer to our steep descent. My black hoodie provided me a safe space to hide as I tucked my head into my chest. Sweat stung my eyeballs as I cowered and trembled while grasping the handlebars for dear life. I was overcome with such fear that I wanted to run, but there was nowhere to go. I lay at the mercy of the handlebars then, just as I lay at the mercy of the nurses now.

Breathe-run-breathe-run.

"Honey, it's okay, we only have to do this once. The sooner we do this, the quicker you get to go and rest. We won't look at you getting undressed. We will hold up these sheets and look away. I know this is weird. We just want to keep you and everyone safe."

A hard knot slid down my throat, making it hard to breathe. My legs remained glued to the ground, eyes forward, brain elsewhere. I pulled my arms through the sleeves of my soft cotton fabric shirt, which slid down onto the floor. Pants and shoes tentatively followed. Still trembling, I removed the last garment of clothing, my yellow duck-print panties.

The nurse started the pat down, and I became as pale as a ghost. *Hurry.*

"Can you turn around? And then we are done."

"Oh, thank god," I said, sighing. I turned around, mooned the nurse, and grabbed the gown to wrap around myself.

"Wait, one more thing!"

"What?"

A fresh pair of blue latex gloves appeared for the last part—the hair screen.

There is nothing on this planet Earth that I hate more than

people touching my hair, especially as a Black woman. I'm not a dog, and I certainly didn't want this woman I didn't know to run her hands through my hair like I was one. Despite my discomfort, I bit the bullet and got it over with. I put my head down and let the nurse scavenge my hair for contraband.

The results were negative. I passed the test.

My normal clothes were taken, and I was given cheap baby-blue hospital scrubs, two pairs of brown padded socks, and a few pairs of paper-thin panties. I was not pleased with the change of attire. *Can't I keep anything of mine to remind me of the life I once had?*

My eyes watered. I couldn't help but wonder: Do *kids* really try to hide objects that are potentially lethal in their hair? I had no intention of ending my life, so this confused me. Before I had time to process my thoughts, I was led into the elevator, accompanied by the nurses to the top floor. When I got off, I was greeted by a tall blond white woman.

"She-lle-th—"

"Shilletha," I quickly corrected her, as I was used to dozens of different mispronunciations of my name.

"Oh, I deeply apologize. You must get that a lot, huh? Well, hey! Come with me. I'm Dr. Rosa. I'm going to be your psychiatrist while you're here with us. Also, you'll have a therapist, and we have medical nurses on-site to distribute medication and who can help if you have any physical needs."

"Okay," I said, as I furrowed my brow and tilted my head to the side, like a dog trying to understand a sound.

"Oh, I'm sorry, Shilletha, do you know what a psychiatrist is?"

I slowly shook my head no. I knew how photosynthesis worked and all fifty states in alphabetical order, but I had no idea what a psychiatrist did. I felt ashamed.

"Sorry, dear. My goal as a psychiatrist is to help find medications that will make you feel less sad and happier—"

"But I'm not sad. I just want to go home and play with Rhyme."

"It's okay, honey, we are here to make sure you're feeling better, and then you'll get to go home and play with your friends again. Okay?"

My eyes watered again as I thought of playing back in the streets, climbing on the monkey bars in Burnham Park.

I wasn't going home.

Rushing Streams Psychiatric Hospital was my first psychiatric hospitalization. Seven pine trees surrounded the tall tan building, giving it a dreadful feel. Three main floors housed patients: the first floor for adults, the third for critical patients, and then there was the second floor—my floor. Eighteen children of different races and origins came together here on the second floor to get better as if our lives depended on it.

Patients were housed together in a "safe and nurturing" environment. Two patients of the same sex shared one room, which had two twin beds, two brown dressers, and a yoga space. Bed frames were bolted to the floor, with no room to play hide-and-seek. Closets were barren of racks and hooks. Doors had lost their knobs. Each room had a tiny window in the corner, as if to allow patients a small space to watch God and pray for a miracle. Staff were on-site 24/7 to support those who needed the comfort of being tucked tightly beneath the cheap, craggy sheets at night, and for those who fought the demons in their heads.

Therapists and psychiatrists shared a hall on the far-right side of the building guarded behind a "key access only" door. There were three psychiatrists who rotated throughout the week, and five therapists who were there on various days including weekends—unlike the psychiatrists, who had weekends off. If someone was admitted on a weekend, they would have to wait until Monday to see a psychiatrist and receive medication unless they were in crisis. Luckily, I arrived on a Tuesday and apparently got one of the nicer doctors.

Adjusting to a new way of life proved trying as days quickly turned into weeks. Privacy was scarce and only granted under certain circumstances. When in our bedrooms, doors were always to remain at least ajar and sometimes even fully open. Exceptions to this rule were only granted when changing clothes or meeting privately with an assigned therapist. Open doors allowed the staff to do safety checks every thirty minutes or so throughout the day and hourly checks at night. Nurses also had the advantage of the "birding hour." As soon as the sun rose, the birds began to sing at the top of their lungs, waking even the deepest sleeper. Monitoring machines rolled down the hall, joining in the natural chorus outside, adding the sounds of their own mechanical chirping. Vitals such as blood pressure, temperature, and heart rate were taken every morning, and sometimes the nurses would throw in an unannounced blood draw. I hated needles, but they seemed to adore them. Needles were the preferred method of administration. If someone had a psychotic break or other severe mental health crisis, nurses would come out running yelling a code name, which they followed up by restraining the patient and injecting them with strong medication in one of their butt cheeks. Seconds later the individual would knock out. It was a truly terrifying sight to see.

I felt like a chick who had been pushed out of her nest. I caught on to the system quickly, but even though I figured it out, I still couldn't help but cry the first few weeks. Crying was viewed as an unstable behavior, and it would be pointless to try and plead your case. Any display of fear, sadness, or anger translated to a longer stay. Tears meant depression and anxiety.

I couldn't comprehend why I was here. I didn't feel any of these things at the time.

Outside, a blacktop "recreation area" lay nearly barren. We were plants starved for sunlight; time outside was precious. One lonely basketball net stood on the right side of the court, with flat balls resting by its feet. A twelve-foot-high wire fence stood between patients and freedom. Escape was impossible, but that didn't stop some from trying. We were kids, but we knew collectively that there was potentially something wrong with each of us—what, we knew not. We wanted out, we wanted to see our parents and friends, we wanted to go to school; we just wanted to be normal kids.

Noelle was the first person I met, a twelve-year-old Black girl whose story broke my heart. Noelle had spent her whole life in various psychiatric hospitals due to schizophrenia. Schizophrenia isolated her from those she needed most in her life. As they were unable to provide a stable life for her, she ended up living here. She was a despondent, withering rose. She was stuck in her own mind—an intricate system of cables and switches that never connected. Her database contained a malware virus that eradicated her master computer system, and no amount of virus protection or computer mechanics could reboot her. Occasionally, she rocked back and forth. Four flat cornrow braids lay parallel on her head, with anchors that dug deeply in her scalp. Her eyes sank into the depths of her skull. They remained dilated and focused, as if she had a relay to be won, but there was no runner to whom she could pass the baton. Her colorless lips were as fragile as a butterfly's wings. Streams of nectar dribbled down her face and collected on her polka-dotted shirt. The nurses would come by every so often with a rough white washcloth to clean her face. Simple tasks and personal hygiene became hurdles for her. One month, when her menstrual cycle started, she seemed unaware of the blood soaking through her pajamas as she walked around in her zombie-like state. A nurse immediately noticed.

"Noelle, honey, why didn't you ask for any sanitary items? Oh my, there is blood all over you, honey. Let's get you cleaned up."

She didn't answer, but tears fell. The nurse guided Noelle down the hall to the private shower area, which was used for those who were disabled by their illness and needed a nurse to help bathe them.

I didn't think Black people could be this way; I had been taught we were much stronger than that. Growing up in the hood and attending Black Baptist churches with my aunt and uncle taught me the greatest rule of mental illness: silence. It wasn't a dinner table topic, and when it was talked about, it was with a very frightening attitude. People like "this" were being attacked by an evil spirit.

Mental illness was a way of thinking and could be "rebuked" out of anyone. Spirits took on names. There was the Spirit of Depression, the Spirit of Anxiety, and so forth, as the Devil only came to kill, steal, and destroy. Hearing voices was demonic in nature and "not of God." If a Black woman suffered from a mental illness, then she was weak. To be weak was exceptional and unacceptable. Our ancestors had gone through endless pain and suffering both physically and mentally throughout slavery and segregation, and thus we, too, had to suck it up and deal with the slippery slope of life. We had to simply shake it off and bring our heavy burdens to the Lord. Why seek the help of a shrink or therapist if you could just talk to Jesus—the greatest counselor of them all? But here I met others who were Black and sick. I couldn't understand why God, who knew everything, couldn't stop people from getting sick like this.

Every evening after dinner, kids were called one by one to the nurse's station to get their nighttime medication. Tiny white paper cups filled with capsules and tablets of blues, greens, and oranges sat behind a tall white desk. One of them was for me. I showed the nurse a white wristband that contained my name, date admitted, weight, and allergens. After I was verified, I grabbed a cup of water from the cooler and swallowed my two drugs: vitamin B and Zoloft. I had heard of Zoloft from TV commercials. They showed a white blob bouncing slowly with a gray cloud hovering drearily over its head. The blob started out with a sad face, but eventually the frown turned upside down—due to the blob taking Zoloft, of course. My frown never turned upside down because I wasn't actually depressed before being taken here. I did cry a lot, however. I also exhibited symptoms such as difficulty sleeping, pessimism, and loss of interest in hobbies, but was that not to be expected?

Hopelessness caught me in its grasp as autumn's falling leaves were silently replaced by winter's snowflakes. The ground had frozen, and the trees became as barren as my spirit. The days and nights bled into each other, and I had no idea how long I'd been here. This whole time, I had not heard from Momma Nan or my aunt and uncle.

"Jingle Bell Rock" echoed from the old boombox in the dayroom, the sound of children's laughter muffled by the tune. *How can anyone laugh and be merry when we are stuck in here?* I thought. Outside, in a world not too far away, families—including mine—were hanging great displays of Christmas lights on their houses and wrapping garlands down banisters. I knew Aunt Barbara would be baking a cake while decorating the Christmas tree. Decorating the tree was my favorite part of Christmas. Ornaments and string lights of every color clung to the artificial branches of our seven-foot tree. At the top we would place a giant white star with the Archangel Gabriel nestled on top. Our Christmas Eve tradition was to attend church in red, gold, or green attire to celebrate Jesus's birthday. Our church usually put on a play with gospel music and reenactments of Mary and Joseph bringing baby Jesus into this world.

But this Christmas had no choirs singing gospel music, no string lights, and not even a Christmas tree. Inside the hospital, staff decorated the halls with pictures of snowmen and paper snowflakes, a poor alternative. Here, Christmas was a distant relative who loved from afar. Patients were given gifts from staff and likely from donors who thought of us during the holidays.

One day, a staff member approached me. "Excuse me, you're Shilletha, right?"

"Um, yeah, I am. Why?"

"A visitor dropped a present off for you. We couldn't let them in because they aren't granted permission. I'm terribly sorry, but hey, they were thinking of you, dear!"

My jaw dropped. *Who sent me something? No one even knows where I am . . . or do they? Maybe it's Rhyme!*

I reached up and grabbed the box, then skipped down the hall back to my room, screaming, "Thanks, miss!"

Back in the safety of my den, nothing could come between the glittery box and me. I knew to some degree that it was simply love in a box, regardless of its contents. I was also aware that the staff had checked the box, as it showed the journey it had gone through: The paper was lacerated at the edges, though perfectly fabricated back together. Anticipation overcame me, and I tore it open. Silky pale-pink pajamas with designs of cupcakes I could only dream of eating lay neatly folded in the white rectangular box.

"Whoa! This is awesome!" I squealed. *But where did this come from?*

Something caught my eye: A piece of paper lay folded along the base of the box. I unfolded it.

It was Aunt Barbara's phone number. Suddenly, I realized that here lay the key to my potential freedom. My mood changed to desperation in a split second. I was a starving lioness who couldn't recall the last time she'd had a hearty meal. The hunger was insatiable. I knew it was time for the hunt, and any mistake could prove fatal.

I need out.

The gift box hit the floor as I ran down the hall to the nurse's station.

"Mister, may I please make a phone call to my aunt?" I pleaded.

"Sure, just make sure you dial the number one before you dial the phone number."

I ran to the wall of booths nearby. It reminded me of jails I saw on the show *Cops*. There were white ugly dividers in between phones. A sign read: PLEASE LIMIT CALLS TO TEN MINUTES. PLEASE BE MINDFUL OF OTHERS.

It was down to the phone and me. This landline was a lifeline to the freedom that I had dreamed of every night. Chills ran down my spine as I picked up the receiver and dialed the numbers.

"Seven . . . three . . . two . . . Wait, don't forget the one. . . ."

One ring followed another for what seemed like an eternity; then, on the last ring, a female voice answered the phone. I went silent for a brief second, then began to speak.

"Hello, Aunt Barbara, this is—"

"MAMA! How are you!? I was so worried. Your grandmother wouldn't tell me where you were. I haven't heard from you in three months, and I knew something was up. She kept you from me! What happened?"

I recounted the events that had happened the day I was admitted to Rushing Streams. My aunt seemed somewhat flabbergasted that my grandmother had put me "in the shrink house," but she had her own take on it. Her theory was that my grandmother's extreme favoritism toward my sister, Ayana, meant she saw me as being disposable.

"It was your grandmother, she didn't want you! She has been trying to keep you away from me! I am so sorry. We will work to get you out of here. This is unbelievable, the blood of Jesus!"

I told her they had put me on a drug called Zoloft, and her tone nose-dived. She was very adamant about me not taking pharmaceutical drugs and instructed me to hide the drug under my tongue or in the depths of my cheeks. My aunt listened to me and validated that there wasn't anything wrong with me. I knew she truly cared about me and my well-being. Sure, I was a troubled kid, but not to the point of being hospitalized. After our twenty-minute conversation, I felt renewed confidence and hope, feelings I had forgotten I could feel.

Afterward, I decided it was time for desperate measures. I ran to the hall looking for my coconspirator. Zachriel, one of the other patients, had taken a liking to me from the start. She was like a little chihuahua with severe anxiety who had a big bark and no bite, and she always asked me to sit by her during dinner. I found her playing Hungry Hungry Hippos alone in the hall.

"Zachriel, I need your help!"

"Girl, what is wrong with you now?"

"My aunt called, and I have been here three whole months! I need to get out of here, she's waiting for me. I don't want to be here anymore. What should I do?"

Zachriel shrugged. "Hmm . . . I dunno. Wait, I got it! Shhh, gotta stay quiet, too many ears around this part of town. Okay, so here's the plan: We gotta escape."

I sat in the corner pondering; my hands had lost their feeling.

"But how in the world are we going to do that?"

"Well, Shilletha, if you just let me finish! Anyway, like I was saying, tomorrow we can climb the fence when the grown-ups aren't looking or create a distraction. We can reach the other side and take off. Then we can take the trains back home."

"Um, okay, but—"

All sounds in the room seemed to quiet as Zachriel's frustration intensified. "There are no *buts* except the one I'm sitting on! Are you with me or not?"

"Fine." I sighed.

The plan was set, and if I wanted out of the hospital I would have to cooperate, even though I had several questions. None of which were answered.

Our plan was set to be executed the next day. Anticipation and adrenaline hit me hard and fast. All night I tossed and turned, swimming in a bed of cold sweat, anticipating the escape. When the sunrise greeted me, I awoke for medication and breakfast with a new sense of optimism. I carried on in a calm and cool way until lunch. But when I was about to be let out for outside time, I was abruptly stopped by a member of staff.

"Shilletha, you're not allowed to go out for recreation time."

Things got quiet. My ears filled with the sound of my throbbing heart. Air became scarce. A large marble slid down the walls of my throat.

"But . . . why?"

The staff member escorted me back to my bedroom and sat me down to explain what had happened. Someone had snitched on me to the staff. Of course, they didn't name the culprit, but Zachriel was the only one who could have known. Betrayal had struck again. I felt it like a knife in my guts as the love in my heart turned to pure hate. My grandmother had already stabbed me, and now Zachriel was finishing the job. I wanted to collapse. Numb but in excruciating pain, I retreated into myself. *Screw her.*

According to staff, the plan had been all my idea. I was now classified as a "high elopement risk," a term they used for those who had a high probability of escaping. From then on, I was to be monitored constantly. My days outside were no more until I regained the trust of the staff. It was unfathomable to think about how I would have to spend an indeterminate number of days cooped up, without the rays of the sun to warm my skin.

Defeated, I lay back on the hard blue pillow. There had to be an end to this madness. All I could do was close my eyes and pray.

Dear Mother God, please lead me through this forest where all I can see is endless treetops and contorted vines but no light to guide me out. Please, angels, help me. In Jesus's name I pray, amen.

I decided that nobody could be trusted. I was determined to follow the rules, stay low, and finish my time as quickly as possible. I didn't need any more attention than what I already had. For the next few days I did just that and followed the routine with finesse. I ate all my meals, which the staff loves when you're hospitalized.

Regular mealtime eating meant that you were on your way to mental wellness. Depressed patients might lose their appetite or purge; those given Seroquel will raid the refrigerator like a stoner, and with Adderall the thought of eating repulses. But routine, "normal" food consumption meant all was well.

Time flew by, and before I knew it two weeks had passed, and they granted me privileges again. It was a snowy Friday when I was once again approached by the same member of the staff who had delivered the news of Zachriel's betrayal and my subsequent punishment.

"Hey, Shilletha, your therapist and team want to meet with you in about an hour. How does that sound?"

What did I do now? Did they find out I have been storing the medication in my cheek? Did Zachriel start her crap again?

I assumed the worst. It was like being called into the principal's office over the intercom and feeling your classmates watch you leave the room. I spent the hour pacing back and forth in my room. When my therapist came for me, I looked into their eyes, searching for hints of what was to come. We walked down the hall behind the keyed door and went into a conference room. On the table lay my file and two blue pens. My therapist spoke first.

"Well, Shilletha, we feel like you have made progress. It's time for you to go home. It'll be on Monday, as we don't do discharges on the weekends. Do you feel that you are ready to go home?"

"Yes! Yes! I am ready!" I nearly jumped out of my seat.

"All right, then. You'll get your things ready on Sunday, and we can go over your discharge papers with your parents or guardians. Everyone here on your team supports this decision, and we are happy to see you go."

I nearly threw up from pure excitement. This weekend would be the last time I would eat yucky breakfast eggs and dry pancakes. This would be the last time I would have to stand in line for medications or be woken up super early for blood draws. This would be the last time I would be confined behind walls. When Monday came and my grandmother arrived to pick me up, all I could do was look at her and wonder, *Why did you do this to me? What did I do? Am I not good enough?*

More unanswered questions.

"How are you doing, Shilletha?" she asked.

"I just want to go play with Rhyme again," I said, not making eye contact with her. She didn't deserve it.

I had gone through so much trauma seemingly for nothing, but I learned one thing from my time at Rushing Streams: They may try to break me, but I can never be broken. Strength was embedded in me the day I arrived on the planet. This setback would actually be a stepping stone.

There was no way I could have known at the time that my very first encounter with the psychiatric system would not be my last, and that my unnecessary hospitalization would soon open the door to a lifetime of struggle with real, debilitating mental illness.

ROAN HIGHLANDS, TENNESSEE

One week and seventy-eight miles after Big Butt Bypass, I stood on the edge of a winding road, deciding whether to proceed three miles northbound to the tent site at Ash Gap or backtrack and set up camp near the road. The sun bade me farewell as she dipped below the horizon. Time was dwindling, and decision-making had never been my strong suit. I debated with myself until the universe had enough. A deep bark echoed through the valley. I looked up and saw a fawn and a black hound dog with no owner in the middle of the road. His hackles were raised like thorns on his back, his eyes narrowed on me. Being the target revived my sense of urgency. I had to move—now.

I trotted calmly across the road, careful not to agitate the fero-
cious beast. I could see the base of the mountain sloping downward
and melding with the earth, calling my name. Although taking
mountains by surprise was my usual approach to the trail—I didn't
want to scare the crap out of myself by staring at the map and
scrolling up the screen to find the summit—I knew it was time to
pull out good old trusty Gothook, the digital guidebook that contained information on water sources, hostels, upcoming towns, trail
goodies, and—my favorite—elevation of the terrain, including an
elevation map of the mountain that stood before me.

There was a steep slope going up, then a series of small ups and
downs that resembled jagged edges of teeth. The trail carved deep
into the side of the mountain as it wound east, then west, and finally
up toward the sky until it reached the Roan High Knob Shelter,
the highest shelter on the Appalachian Trail at over 6,000 feet.
Thankfully, my destination that night, Ash Gap, was only halfway.
Darkness motivated me to gallop through the forest. When I finally
reached the tent site, I could barely make out the two figures in
the distance among the city of trees. I recognized one man's voice.

"Skellington!" I sighed in relief that tonight I would not be
sleeping alone.

Skellington, an older man in his seventies but youthful at heart,
and I had been leapfrogging each other on the trail. I could never
seem to escape his raspy voice and good humor. Many years ago he
had taken a fall from a ladder and nearly severed his vocal cords, and
now he was thru-hiking the Appalachian Trail. He was unstoppable,
a freight train at full speed, stopping only to catch relief sprawled out

in the grass. With good company and plenty of weed to go around, I set up camp and enjoyed the night with Skellington. Tomorrow would bring sweat, blood, and tears.

The next day the sawtooth mountain stood before me, looming in the distance, soaring high above the land, kissing the heavens in a cloud of cool mist. After saying goodbye to Skellington, I cautiously edged down the path, crumbling delicate twigs beneath the weight of my feet. I looked up in awe at the canopies of the giants shielding me from my demons. My footsteps became a heartbeat, pulsing through the forest, feeding my body with fresh blood. Sweat settled on my face like morning dew, stinging my sleepy eyes. For hours, I weaved through the mountain, becoming one with it as I ascended higher into the blue heavens, the cool wind caressing my face, the wispy cirrus clouds dashing through the air around me. A calming song erupted from a black gum tree where birds basked in the sun. I sang along to the catchy tunes, chirping in harmony with the flock as I reached the summit. The ghostly mist had lifted, and the peak was bestowed with a tiara of powdery white snow and sleek sheets of rock-solid ice. Rays of light bloomed through the forest like petals of a sunflower. I took a moment to be present and gave thanks to the land around me before descending the back side of the mountain.

"Thank you, nature, for providing this space. Thank you, trees, bees, and seeds."

As I made my way down, the trail was starkly different from the north side, barren of soil but abundant with pebbles, gravel, and loose rock. Quickly, I became frustrated with the monotonous mountain and plugged my headphones into my ears, racing to a road that was within my grasp. Peering through the trees, I saw the road and a hideous chestnut-brown-and-white sign that said CARVER'S GAP. Cars lined the parking lot and spilled into the road as if a football game was about to push off. Day hikers roamed around like chickens, pecking for worms, oblivious to the Appalachian Trail they were walking on. This gap was the gateway to the Roan Highlands, a five-mile stretch of grassy mountain balds straddling the state line of Tennessee and western North Carolina. I had never heard of a bald before that moment, let alone known what I was hiking into. How could this be? Mountains without trees in America? My own country was foreign to me; I had been blind to its wonders.

Open fields of hay danced in the wind, each prickly blade shining in the sunlight. The mountains, a bold testament to time, rose upward like lighthouses, their beacons guiding wandering souls. Jagged rocks pierced my hiking boots as I staggered up Round Bald. Harmony existed here between the elements, cruel yet bountiful, punishing yet rewarding. That was the true nature of nature. Everything had checks and balances: Where I'd find pain, there was joy; where there was poison ivy, the antidote lay nearby. I was infatuated. I stood upon the bosom of the earth, tears welling up in my eyes. Neither grief nor sadness overcame me. The mountains humbled me and made me feel small, so infinitely insignificant, a feeling that was foreign to me. I had discovered the temple to a lost heaven, one I had spent my life searching for.

I headed up to Jane Bald, my home for the night. I had walked a measly five miles from my last tent site, but I was a sucker for setting up camp at breathtaking sites. Earlier, I had come across a hiker who said that he never stayed in a shelter on a trail, only stealth-camped in cool places. "You should give it a try sometime." The idea stuck to me like sweet honey, but the fear stung me like a bee. *Will I be safe? What if a man comes and attacks me? What if nobody finds my body?* I pictured a black bear standing before me, ready to charge, her broad paws swatting at the dirt, her glossy eyes watching mine. Every nerve in my body telling me to run, but I'd stand my ground, for if I ran, I'd be dead. Fear had forged me into a fighter. Out in the wild, I was a predator myself, equipped with a blade and a three-ounce mace canister.

This wasn't my first night camping solo, but each time felt as if it were the first. Nature hissed at me, exhaling with all her might. I tussled with the stubborn wind, trying to calm its emotions, but it whipped my tent up and over my head, forcing me to hold on to the tent's legs, surrendering to its will. Without trees on the bald there was nothing to stop the wind's brute force. I never took trees for granted again.

When the wind finally became weary, I staked my tent, pushing firmly down with my shoe and gathering rocks for reinforcement. Pleased by my invention, I found a rock outcropping that provided a decent place to start dinner. I gorged myself on a double helping of chicken ramen, lapping up every delicate noodle from every crevice of the camp pot. After I had my fill, I gazed out into the distance.

Nature sprawled out before me. I sat beside her, naked as she was, a spectator in her kingdom. Mountains stood in every corner of the earth, surrounding me. Dusk whispered like strokes of an artist's brush, her lavender and amber hues cutting through the blazing orange setting sun. I opened my eyes as she closed hers. For years, I had been asleep in the world, blinded and led astray, plugged into a matrix.

I had been bound by the chains of capitalism, forced to choose between pursuing the passions that fed my soul or staying stagnant and starving, grappling every day to find happiness. Now I knew that everything outside of the forest was an illusion, a fictional world where humans were like Sims being controlled by the confines of society, forced to acclimate to a civilization that was sucking their souls. I, too, had fallen victim to the curse, but it was time to break the spell. Hiking was my salvation; the forest, my church; and the mountains, my god. The peace allowed me to unlock my inner self, walking through doorways that had once been barricaded. It suddenly dawned on me that I was officially hiking the Appalachian Trail. The windows to heaven opened, and I saw eternity, a promise of life twinkling in the perfect blackness.

In the morning on Jane Bald, I made two packets of apple-cinnamon oatmeal, trail style, by adding the boiling hot water to the paper bag. Water sometimes seeped out at the corners, but it was better than doing dishes. No one liked doing dishes on trail; I barely liked doing them at home.

The first couple of hours of hiking in the morning were my favorite time of day, even as I struggled to leave my tent by nine thirty a.m. most days. In those hours, my strength was at its greatest and my mind was just as sharp. I walked with my eyes fixed on the trail. As I hiked, I felt invincible, and a new determination rose in me. Maybe it was a good night's rest. Maybe it had been the stars, rocking me to sleep. Maybe, this particular time, it had been my confrontation with myself on Big Butt Bypass. Whatever it was, it had me dancing and clacking my trekking poles up the mountain.

Hiking the AT was not the biggest challenge I had faced in my life. Yes, there was the torrential rainfall and the soul-draining heat, the raw bunions that would later develop on the sides of my pinky toes that slid against the padding of my oversized shoes, the thirst and the insatiable hunger, exhaustion and deprivation, the angels and the demons that haunted and anointed me with holy water as I planned to walk all 2,193 miles from Georgia to Maine. The thing was, I had already gone through much worse before the AT, and I knew that just like the moon would always take the place of the sun in the sky, more was to come.

I just had to be prepared.

6

WANING GIBBOUS

The school guidance counselor's office became a place of familiarity as I failed to readjust to the routine that had been interrupted many moons ago by the hospitalization. By eighth grade, I had been through six different schools. Custody battles among my aunt, grandmother, and mother bounced me between the cities of Morristown, Newark, and Manchester and ushered in an extreme change in my behavior. Gaps in curricula between schools and from absences had a drastic effect on my education.

I had already been unofficially diagnosed with dyscalculia, which impeded my ability to do basic math. Decimals, fractions, and even the lines on a twelve-inch ruler were foreign to me. Knowing that I struggled, my aunt took me to Sylvan Learning Center, where they tested me and told me that all hope was lost because I was at a fifth-grade math level. The schools' predominantly white teachers failed me just as they failed many Black kids around the country. Preconceived notions that we were not capable of learning coupled with stereotypes and the devastating effects of an entrenched system of discrimination stunted our education and opportunities right from the jump. Asking for help or for an opportunity was met with great resistance. But that was the narrative for so many of us, especially in the hood. And when other kids started to pick on me, that narrative didn't budge.

I was first bullied in Morristown in elementary school starting around age seven, and the ostracization spread contagion-like throughout the rest of elementary school. On top of my learning disabilities, I also stood out physically. An ocular pigment condition dotted the whites of my eyes with a bluish hue. Cruel children dubbed me "alien girl" and accused me of rubbing blue ink from pens in my eyes to give myself a "tattoo." In middle school, hate notes were frequently slipped into my locker for me to find between classes. Many were filled with statements about how ugly I was.

You are so ugly.

Dark ugly alien girl.

No one likes you because you have cooties.

I cried because I believed them. Yeah, I was ugly, and who would want to be friends with an ugly, dark-skinned, almost-hairless girl? I hated myself and wondered if, like Shrek in the sequel, maybe one day I, too, might find the secret potion to be beautiful like the other girls my age. Apparently, that's how hideous I was.

Eventually I couldn't bear the cruel remarks anymore and ended up back with my mother in the Newark public school system. Newark schools were scary to me, as they were over-policed, and we were forced to go through metal detectors every day. We weren't criminals, and I hated being treated like one simply because the school was in the hood. Many of our teachers were white and had no understanding of our struggles or any desire to teach us.

As the years went by, the classroom transformed into a battleground. There were fights between students at every opportunity, and sometimes for no reason at all. During one particular fight, a quiet, heavyset girl in class was singled out and pounced on like a zebra by a pride of lions. Out of nowhere, another girl began to scream and yell, calling her a "fat bitch" and "a hoe." Shortly thereafter, a second bully joined the commotion, punching the poor girl in her face and pulling the girl's weave right out of her scalp. Of course, all the students gathered round, amplifying the ordeal with their ruckus. I felt bad, but I was also an object of derision because I "spoke like a white girl."

Aunt Barbara always told me I spoke properly and to never, ever be ashamed of sounding educated because I didn't "talk that hood talk." Aunt Barbara told me that a Black woman who spoke in slang was seen as loud and confrontational, which was what white people expected when they looked at us, as if we were untamed animals. She believed that the way I spoke would enable me to fit into white America, carving me a pathway to success. Whiteness in America was the American dream. When you were white, you got privileges. When you "sounded white" and had a "white-sounding name" as a Black woman, it made white people think you were capable of learning and had a good head on your shoulders. It got you interviews quicker than if you spoke in Ebonics or had a name like Shilletha. Growing up, I was taught to embrace whiteness and push away Blackness.

My peers continued to taunt me, positing that I "thought I was better than everyone else because I talked like a white girl." My speech was such a point of contention that it got me thrown into a glass wall once. I remember just looking up and thinking, *What did I do wrong?*

I stuck to myself and my studies, which was also considered a "white activity." My only friends were my blue-striped pencil, my folder with pink cartoon ponies on the cover, and the work that was handed to me. Burned-out teachers merely sat, hot-glued to their desks, and babysat the students, as their work was cut out for them. Teaching impoverished Black and Brown children who barely had structure in their homes, who had no discipline and a host of intergenerational emotional and psychological traumas, seemed nearly impossible. A lot of my classmates were just as poor as I was and lacked proper social skills. Attention-seeking behavior was common, but how could it not be? Without the proper foundation that a child was supposed to receive from their parents, when chaos was surging back home, how were they supposed to be present in class?

Even though I received high marks in history, English, science, and music class, the physical bullying did not end. Symptoms of ADHD started to shine their light onto my world. Teachers would constantly call me out in class for drifting off into a world unknown to them. When they tried to explain the way things worked, I would make eye contact throughout the conversation but could never keep my mind present.

I knew nothing about ADHD, and no one got me tested. After all, I was a young child, and back then this was "normal" behavior. Even if I wasn't born fiending for a substance I couldn't conceptualize, marked by mental and development delays—including ADHD. Medical experts would note that later in life the effects of maternal cocaine use could still be seen in a range of impairments, from physical to cognitive. Most commonly, attention to tasks, information processing, and planning were affected. As noted earlier, my mother denies using crack while pregnant with me.

Without a diagnosis, I still excelled in my studies, except for math, as usual. I graduated from elementary school with a few honorable mentions: Student of the Month and Awards of Excellence for adapting to one school after a move. Aunt Barbara even brought me a Shih Tzu puppy, whom I named Tigger, because I was doing so well. But the toll of the shuffling, struggling, and bullying was still present, and I ended up with an assigned guidance counselor in seventh grade to help sort things out.

Mrs. Willow was a lady of medium stature with the neck of a giraffe and the personality of a Newfoundland. Her rounded glasses took up most of her square face, and her teeth couldn't be contained in her mouth. However, this was no laughing matter.

"Shilletha, I have been very concerned about you. Someone who also cares about you informed me that you have been self-harming and cutting yourself."

By this point, wounds covered me. My arms and legs had stick drawings engraved in them. I had charged my friend Gina with anchoring this secret, but she had let the ship sail. I couldn't fault her, though, because she just wanted me to be safe. Every day she would grab my arms, roll up my sleeves, and sometimes even slap my cuts in an attempt to get me to stop. Little did she know how addictive and strong the urges were to see self-inflicted blood, something I had only started to give in to recently. It was the cigarette I had never thought I would smoke.

"Shilletha, have you been cutting yourself?" Mrs. Willow repeated.

"Well, uh, yeah."

"Can you tell me a little more about what has been going on?"

I really can't. "I'm dealing with a lot . . ."

"Dealing with what? I know it's hard to talk about this, but I am here to help you. We care about you here, and so does your friend. We just want to keep you safe, is all."

To expose the truth would mean exposing myself, a turtle without a shell. I did not fully comprehend the concept of "my truth" at this young age. Truth was supposed to set one free, but I didn't know if I was ready to fly. Do or die. Finally, I relented.

"Um. Mrs. Willow?"

"Yes, Shilletha."

"There is—a person. A man . . ."

"It's okay, tell me."

"At my house . . ."

He only came out at night.

One night, when my mother was out and my sisters were in bed, he lured me into the living room. On the TV, WWE fighters Rey Mysterio and Eddie Guerrero were taking on Heartbreak Kid Shawn Michaels. The Heartbreak Kid's theme song played in the background, muffling my unease.

"Relax, you're too tense. But I know what will help."

Pain paralyzed me for what seemed like an eternity. I finally heard the front doorknob turn and someone entered. The world stopped. Time stood still.

I heard a sharp whisper. "Go to your room." Shame and guilt overcame me as I squished my face into the comfort of my old pillow. Pictures of the R&B singer Ashanti remained where I had left them stuck on the wall to the right of my bed. And there were my sisters, fast asleep and blissfully unaware of the events that had transpired. Eventually I dozed off, too.

Mental anguish stalked me like a shadow for the next few weeks. I needed someone who could listen to me and do something. What if this was happening to my sister and his daughter as well? I immersed myself in the depths of books, *I Spy* and *Where's Waldo*. Waldo was lucky that he could vanish in a crowd but be found by hundreds of children. And there I was, unseen, unheard, and more alone than I had ever felt. It was time to take a stand. I was terrified, but there were other lives at risk. I decided to tell my grandmother when I landed back at her house. My feet were glued to the floor, and I felt as if I had duct tape over my mouth. But I didn't falter. I spoke the truth.

"Momma Nan. Something happened at my mother's house. Something bad."

"Bad like what, Shilletha?"

"Really bad. With my mother's boyfriend."

"Did he put his hands on you? It's okay, you can tell me the truth."

"Yes."

I could see my grandmother's jaw clench.

My grandmother told the police. The word traveled fast and there were some in my family who thought I should let it go. "Shilletha, don't say anything to these cops," I was told.

"But it really happ—"

"Just say it was a mistake and you forgive him."

"But it did happen."

But what if I don't forgive him?

Because I didn't.

Elephants join together and form a circle around their calves to protect them from danger. But gazelles continue to run away even if a predator catches their fawn, unable to protect their young. Did I live among elephants or gazelles? I had to save myself. The lesson I was beginning to learn was that my life was not valuable to others. I thought Black girls mattered, but Black girls like me were silenced for speaking up. Talking about things like this was like trying to stop an infectious disease from spreading. It wasn't that my family wasn't aware; it was that they wanted to keep it a secret, and now I was a leper. But I had felt like a leper since birth, so what was the difference?

When I went to meet with the prosecutor in a dark wood-paneled room, she said, "Shilletha, I heard you like to draw, is that right?"

"Yes," I said, wiggling in my seat.

"We got you a canvas and some crayons. Go at it."

Art provided a blank slate to draw my emotions, feelings, and expressions. I drew the outline of a dog during the investigative interview. Angel wings and a halo completed the picture as I self-soothed. This was Zaxo, the guardian angel dog I had made up in my own creative world. They asked me questions for a full hour. Now what?

He ended up going to jail. Meanwhile I felt like a failure. I had taken a father away from his young daughter. But he had stolen my life in ways neither of us could have imagined. Childhood trauma wreaks havoc throughout the developing brain, leaving scars that carry into adulthood. It affects our ability to think. It impairs learning and problem-solving. It constantly puts us into survival mode. Simply put, I was fucked. My brain was no longer under my control. My body was tainted, and no matter how hard I scrubbed, I would always feel dirty. Even though I was only twelve years old, I knew my childhood was lost forever. While he went to jail, I endured a sentence of my own as the trauma locked me behind bars that physically could not be broken. No amount of fire or force could break me out as the pain persisted.

The experience left an indelible mark on me. I was now part of a statistic: that one in four women experience rape, molestation, or sexual assault. I was one of many Black girls silenced until adulthood. Black communities tend to take a passive approach to abuse, reluctant to address its perpetrators and repercussions, an effect of systemic oppression. In the Black community, the attributes of a "collectivist culture" see most of us sacrificing the interests of the individual for what is in the best interest of the group because the group—family, tribe, or state—is the principal element of reality.

This is a setup for failure, notable in the effects of unaddressed trauma. Kids who are affected act out in school, displaying symptoms and developing anxiety, PTSD, and the like because they are expected to stay silent. Some of these children, especially Black boys, will eventually end up in juvenile detention or prison because they are unable to regulate their emotions. They turn to fighting, gangs, or selling drugs because of undiagnosed mental disorders, neglect, and lack of family structure and environmental stability. It's often not until adulthood that victims seek therapy and treatment, if they do at all.

My home life never went back to normal. Even then, my normal wouldn't have been anyone else's normal. Countless arguments, screaming, yelling, and physical punishments were common. In some Black families, the rod was a frequent guest that came in different forms: belts, switches, hands, and rulers. There were no reservations or escape from a good ass-whuppin'. Beatings came for an array of reasons. You could count on a beating if you "stepped out of line," talked back, or didn't respect your elders. Other times, beatings broke up sibling fights, came after school failings, or punished not waking up for church on Sunday morning. This abuse was commonplace and a cultural norm in my community, but whatever the reason and regardless of its effectiveness, I hated being hit. Once, I was in the bathtub when my grandmother came in and started beating me with a belt for "stealing" my friend's Game Boy when my friend had told me that I could borrow it. Her mother had called after school to say that Charlotte was sobbing because I had taken her game. Charlotte was white, and her mother had no tolerance for a thief. No one would believe me, and so I paid the price in skin.

A combination of environment, genetics, trauma, family structure, and instability in housing are the building blocks for mental disorders. The cards were not in my favor. My father died of AIDS before I got a chance to know him. My mother told me that he was a military man who struggled with depression. My father's genes play a role in my physical appearance and personality, no doubt, but they may also have left traces of him deeper within me. Psychiatric disorders run in families. Autism, ADHD, bipolar disorder, major depression, and schizophrenia are all thought to have a genetic component.

Aunt Barbara told me that in my father's final days, he started going to church and gave his life to Jesus. His favorite song was "Let Everything That Has Breath" by Ron Kenoly, a Black gospel singer. Every now and then I thought about what he might have been like, and I wondered if he was watching over me.

Though my world became a dark and dangerous place, I never faltered. I took with me a precious lesson: Never again did I want to become a victim. I was *not* a victim; I was a survivor. I kept attending school, sang in the children's choir at church, and hung out with my cousins every weekend. I kept busy to deal with the internal adversity. I didn't even know therapy was an option.

I was taught that if you forgive, God will always forgive you. I felt as if I only had two choices: forgive and adapt—or die. My choice was to adapt.

DAMASCUS, VIRGINIA

The "Virginia Blues" is what thru-hikers call it. Long as balls—the longest stretch on the AT—this state is seen by many as an obstacle, while others embrace its beauty and brutality. Five hundred and thirty-one miles of rolling hills, colorful meadows, arduous climbs, and elegant pastures were divided into two sections: southern Virginia and northern Virginia. The Appalachian Trail saunters into southern Virginia from the Cherokee National Forest in Tennessee, crossing the state line to the long-awaited milestone of the quaint and hiker-friendly town of Damascus, Virginia.

This town holds one of the hidden treasures of the AT, an experience nearly every thru-hiker wants to be a part of. For three days in early May, the town becomes a vibrant city, packed with homes of nylon, polyester, and Cuben Fiber, homes that move and walls that ripple in the wind. Hikers swarm the town during peak season like a school of fish, eagerly waiting to be fed and, quite frankly, to party, trip, and drink themselves into oblivion. No one is a freak here; we are all one and the same—stinky thru-hikers, with one goal on our mind: Katahdin. How we get there is our choice, but along the way, a little partying never hurts. For this reason, the Appalachian Trail has earned a reputation as the party trail. Packing out six-packs of Pabst Blue Ribbon and Coors is common, calories with a slight boost. Weed, acid, and mushrooms are gentle pleasantries taken to enhance the connection with nature.

Trail days like these, however, were not a possibility for me at the time in 2021 given the raging coronavirus pandemic and the possibility of contracting it. I arrived in Damascus a week after the festivities had ceased. It was mid-May, the fresh blooms of spring in the air. Crossing my third state line was an accomplishment, and I welcomed Virginia with an open mind and heart. Being infatuated with state lines was common on the trail, and I noticed many hikers took to the trail like a racehorse and measured their accomplishments by how fast they powered through the states, boasting about the high mileage they had done.

But speed had no effect on my morale; I knew every hundred miles would yield surprises waiting for me. The trail always provided. For myself, I knew I would get to wherever it was when I would. I had everywhere to go and nowhere to be. And so I followed the winding trail out of the lush forest and into the streets of Damascus, white blazes displayed on the prominent electric poles.

Walking through town gave me a confidence boost. Knowing I was a thru-hiker went to my big fat head at times, and I wanted the locals to know who I was and where I was going. Many locals kissed the sweet ground I walked on as a thru-hiker.

"You're a thru-hiker? No way! That has always been my dream."

"You're my hero."

Hearing the voices of white people telling me I was their hero baffled me. I had been called a nigger, a coon, dirty, and more . . . but never a hero.

I had never been anyone's hero or even considered myself a hero. Heroes have always been firefighters, nurses, and my favorite Marvel character, Iron Man. I damn sure wasn't Iron Man. I never saved the day. I didn't have high-tech gadgets or surgical tools to fix a tethered body. There was no metal suit, just flesh and blood. I was a meatsuit. All I had were twenty-five pounds on my back and two feet that would carry those twenty-five pounds in pain and in plea-sure for 2,193 miles. Nothing in my life seemed heroic or worthy of celebration. Yet I was pursuing a dream that only one Black woman had achieved before. I had survived sexual abuse. I was turning my pain into power. I was climbing mountains. I had defeated the odds. With each step, I developed self-control, empathy, and the ability to make critical decisions when faced with nature's wrath.

I was hiking through states that had deep roots in slavery and the Civil War, and that was no easy feat. Virginia was one of those states, but thankfully, I soon discovered I wasn't alone.

In Damascus, I stayed in a popular hostel called the Broken Fiddle. Every other hostel had been booked up, including the local church open to house hikers for free. In front of the hostel, nine narrow sea-green wooden planks were plastered on a six-foot wood post. Navy-green arrows were painted meticulously on each plank, their noses acting as compasses, pointing in the directions of different locations. The mileage of the landmark rested above the arrow. These signs were extraordinary. I examined the names of towns and notable mountains and landmarks. MCAFEE KNOB: 242.8, SPRINGER MOUNTAIN: 470.8, and KATAHDIN: 1721.2 MILES. Reading the mileage comforted me. I, Dragonsky, had walked 470.8 miles as a solo woman, a feat that concerned most women due to the danger and presence of strange men. I had inherited a temper and a strong will to defend myself. In fact, being solo gave me independence, the ability to rely on myself, and the freedom to hike my hike the way I wanted to.

The old chestnut house behind the sign had faded with time. A bench barricaded the front door. Access denied; there had to be another way in. I scoured the yard to figure out the puzzle. Had there been no hikers on the porch, I would have thought it to be vacant.

"Hey, are you looking for the entrance? You gotta go down to your right where the mural is. Go through that fence," a hiker called out.

"Thanks!"

I skipped across the grass and unhooked the latch leading to the backyard. The wide wooden door swung ajar, and I was met with eager and curious eyes. On the covered patio, white string lights glistened along the ceiling and worn couches from last year's garage sale gave personality to the space. There was an artistic touch to it, a rustic beauty, a versatility that I loved. A single hammock swing swayed gently in the wind, anchored to the ceiling in the back corner, and behind it were a field of lush, velvety grass and a single tent that belonged to Treehouse, a former AT thru-hiker who had started the Broken Fiddle and who lived on the property. His shaggy beard and kind spirit filled the hostel. He worked hard, doing hikers' laundry, making sure operations were smooth and that we were enjoying ourselves. Impressed, I purchased a bunk, got the rundown of the rules, and settled in for the night for a double zero. A zero is a day off trail, but taking just one day off always seemed foolish to me. My body needed more than one day to recover, and I strictly adopted the double zero policy.

The next day, my stomach, ravenous, woke me up. It was my duty to satisfy and control its rage. Hikers raved about the Damascus Diner in town; apparently it had stellar food, and it was cheap as dirt. What true New Jerseyan could resist the allure of a diner when we were the diner capital of the world? I made my way down to the diner with some hikers I had gotten acquainted with overnight. I ordered a scrumptious meal of two strips of bacon, three scrambled eggs, and one savory pancake. As we waited for our food, I turned and noticed another group sitting on my left.

A white woman and three Black girls. My world came to a halt.

Had my eyes deceived me? Were there really three young Black girls thru-hiking the AT? They certainly didn't live here, I thought. Southern Virginia wasn't like Alexandria or the DMV area. It wasn't a welcoming place for us; all the other faces surrounding me were white. My eyes never strayed, glued to the children, but I couldn't gather the courage to introduce myself.

If it's meant to be, our paths will cross again.

The next morning, I grabbed my gear and got back on the trail. Leaving town, the Appalachian Trail climbs for a series of pointless ups and downs while the blue blazes stay low to follow the Virginia Creeper Trail and reconnect later with the AT, avoiding unnecessary bullshit. The option to go around the white blazes and discover new adventures always appealed to me, but some look on such deviation with disgust. Purists follow every white blaze to perfection, being meticulous to backtrack any mile lost to a hitch or a hindrance on the trail. White blazes are viewed as sacraments, marking the true route, and to miss any white blaze is blasphemy. Punishable by who? Well, that's a grand mystery. I didn't know there were rules to the trail, nor did I care. White blazes marked the trail, and that was simply the road; it didn't mean I couldn't venture down other avenues. My only rule was maintaining a continuous footpath from terminus to terminus, blue blaze or white blaze—who gives a fuck. The trail got a bit redundant at times; it needed some spice. I needed a change of scenery. It was time to creep onto a new trail.

The creek babbled under a series of bridges, accompanying me down the bustling paved path. Smooth pebbles were whisked about in the underwash, sparkling like rubies under strings of soft light. Creeks and rivers contain the true soul of the wilderness. It moved me like the subtle sweep of a painter's brush, distracting me from the distant bells of bicyclists and the engines of cars. The mountains silently observed in the background, guarding their secrets within. Virginia Creeper, a deciduous plant, dominated the trail. Arcing into the air, bees hovered over the vine, performing the ballet of the creek with sticky yellow slippers. I enjoyed the sights of nature in motion for a moment, knowing the white blazes were within reach. Then it was time to return to the main course and get to my first landmark in Virginia—the Grayson Highlands.

Getting there meant summiting Virginia's highest peak, Mount Rogers. Climbing Mount Rogers doesn't stick out in my memory; to me it was just another mountain, another challenge to conquer. The names of mountains I do not hold dear, but the ones that wanted me to know them called out to me. Every mountain has a soul, an energy that lingers like the morning mist on its crown, but only a few shared a connection with me. Virginia didn't call out to me. But it did push me out of my comfort zone.

By no means was it easy. The mountains held a vengeance against me, busting my calves on every ascent as my muscles pulsed and screamed. Stretching every morning became a routine to loosen up my body and get it ready for each climb. My first day in the Grayson Highlands proved to be especially brutal. The temperature dropped from fifty to eighteen degrees in a matter of four hours, triggering a minor snowstorm and a decline in the possibility of seeing the wild ponies. Everyone talked about the ponies in the Grayson Highlands, but I couldn't care less; it was cold, windy, and downright miserable. Thank the great nature gods that I had studied the weather in southern Virginia before my hike. May was unpredictable, and winter still held on like a silent ghost, looming in the distance. I had come prepared with my zero-degree mitts and my puffy coat, which I never sent home. Adapt, die, or go home—and I was always ready to adapt.

The next few days, I hiked under tunnels of rhododendron. The epitome of spring, they delighted the forest in full bloom. Cows grazed the meadows and occasionally blocked the cattle gates I had to unlock to continue on the trail. Their presence intimidated me. Their broad bodies and menacing stares tracked my every movement like they were nurses on suicide watch. I'd converse with them as I scooted around, hoping they would take my bargain to have mercy on me rather than charge and trample me into the ground. Cows weren't always harmless.

I was ten miles before the mile 545 marker at the road that led to Newport, Virginia, when I found my bear sack had only two Clif Bars left. Unbeknownst to me, I had been running a day short on food. Desperate, I pulled out Guthooks, pressing on icons, hoping that they would give me some direction. There was almost always a trail angel or shuttle in the area that could take me to a convenience store four miles or so down the road. I found the name of a trail angel and texted her. Although there were notes in the map that there was no service at the road, we connected and confirmed for a pickup at five p.m. that evening. With plans solidified, I cast my worries to the wind, ate my bars, and got to the road at a quarter to five.

Several cars drove by. I waited anxiously on the edge of the road, hoping to see her car. No one came. An hour passed, and I frantically begin texting the trail angel through my Garmin safety device, only to receive nothing. The evening sun cast long shadows on the pavement, the moon rising up to relieve her. Accepting the fact that she had flaked on me, I put my pack back on and stuck my right thumb out.

Every white hiker had simply told me, "Just hitch." Everything on trail was dependent on the kindness and wheels of others. But hitching in Virginia as a Black woman, in a state that had enslaved 550,000 Africans and most notably enforced Jim Crow laws in Shenandoah National Park, leading to the segregation of the park, sent chills down my spine.

Five minutes later, a black SUV pulled up. A white man in his late forties.

"Do you need a ride? Where are you headed to?" he asked.

"Uh, I just need to go down the street to the convenience store," I said.

"Okay, no problem. I can give you a ride, jump in." His tone was flat and lackluster, eyes hidden behind his shades.

We said nothing to each other except "Thank you" and "You're welcome" once we reached the store. Out front, two cars had T-boned each other, causing quite a scene of nosy onlookers. I hurried inside, hoping to dodge any interactions. I looked around, astounded by the packages of Knorr sides, ramen noodles, cold bottled drinks, and sleeves of snacks, feeling high on the anticipation of satisfying my appetite.

I purchased two packs of chicken-flavored ramen noodles, two sleeves of Ritz crackers, a bag of Lays, and one liter of Smartwater.

Outside, a blond man leaning on his dilapidated 1970s Buick watched from afar as I unpacked my pack, cramming the food contents inside. He walked toward me and halted, just close enough to reach out and touch my shoulder.

"Are you a thru-hiker?"

"Yes," I said.

"My name is Connor. Are you looking for a ride back to the trail?"

"Maybe . . ." I hesitated.

"I can bring you back. And what do you say to some KFC I have in the back seat? I know you must be hungry, all those miles you've hiked."

I stared at him for a few seconds, a series of thoughts and feelings rushing over me in waves—grateful for his offer but scared as hell. On the rear side of his car, another white man appeared, looked at me, and offered reassurance. "My man Connor, he's a good guy. You have nothing to worry about."

I accepted his offer. I got into the passenger seat, the only bare spot of car available. The inside of the car was filled with boxes, and it reeked of cigarette smoke. An open can of Coors Light rested in the cupholder in the middle, and it was not empty. I put my pack on the filthy floor, my legs resting on top of it. Connor came back, toting a six-pack of beer, waved goodbye to his comrade, and sat in the driver seat. As we drove off, the man sipped on his beer as he asked me question after question and went on and on about his own life growing up.

"So, when you thinking of finishing the AT?"

"I don't know? I like to take my—"

"There's a lot of thru-hikers this year. Seen 'em myself," he interrupted.

"Yeah." I just nodded.

Finally, he pulled the car over at the trailhead, where we grabbed the chicken. It was already dark by this time, and I was not looking forward to getting back on the trail to find shelter for the night.

"You wanna beer and a joint?" He winked.

"Yeah, why not? Calories are a hiker's best friend. And a little bit of Mary J couldn't hurt."

As we indulged, he offered up his place to stay for the night. I could pitch the tent in his yard. It was dark, and I was exhausted. Plus, he mentioned that he had a wife and a daughter at home. The presence of women in his house was a relief. And it was only a five-minute drive from the trailhead, I reasoned, so if anything went wrong, I could easily reach the trailhead on foot. I typically lived by Murphy's Law: "Anything that can go wrong will go wrong."

He asked if I was hiking alone. When I said yes, my answer seemed to concern him.

"It's not good to be alone out there as a woman. It probably gets really cold, and you have no man to cuddle up with. You know, as long as you don't lie with a woman. God said men should not lie with men as a man lies with a woman. I live by that. My daughter's gay. I don't get it; it's a sin, but I love her, ya know. I got to."

What the actual fuck. Don't comment. Just nod.

There were words I wished to say, words I chose not to say. The right words would have given me refuge while the wrong ones would have gotten me left on the side of this country road. Sometimes in nature there are no good moves; the obstacle you resist the most is the one you must surrender to. It was my first time accepting such an offer from a stranger where I felt so uncomfortable, and I was completely at a loss for how to respond or react in a way that would keep me safe.

When we arrived at the house, he grabbed my gear and led me in. There, he introduced me to his wife.

"Oh, you must be so tired and hungry. I'm so sorry the house is a mess, I didn't know you were coming. I'll grab my daughter, and she can make you something," she said, unaware of the KFC bucket sitting on the counter. Before she could leave, Connor cut her off.

"Are you fucking kidding me?! Y'all are trying to cook her something when I brought all this fried chicken home?" His tone became deeper, a sharp contrast to the soft, jolly man I had met back at the store. She didn't say anything, and he didn't reply. They fell into silence as if they were at a rock concert, the volume too loud to conversate, the effort too much to bother with.

I took a seat on the couch, the yellow light of the lamp grazing my face.

Connor approached me, his voice cheery and warm again. "So, do you still want to sleep outside in your tent, or take the couch?"

"I'm not sure—"

My words were abruptly cut off as someone entered the living room.

"This is my daughter, Sage," the wife said.

Sage looked to be around my age, but her narrow hazel eyes were an elderly woman's, lovely but ancient, a reflection of all that she'd endured. A story—our story—was painted on both of her wrists; her world had been shattered more than once. Pity filled my heart. We were both lesbians, both sinners. She kept to herself, seemingly avoiding Connor at all costs. We introduced ourselves briefly, and she retreated to her room.

Connor hastily walked out of the back hall and through the front door to check out my tent. I had set my tent up when we arrived, just to be safe if danger were to arise. I remained in the living room, watching the wife pull up multiple browser windows on her laptop. She worked in silence. A twin bed with floral bedding stood at the right of her desk in the living room, which I found strange. On the left wall, a cabinet polished in wood finish and two large windows revealed a pharmacy. *Whose drugs are those?*

There were three rooms in the house, and it seemed each person slept within their own confines. I had questions. I was a detective, scoping out clues, struggling to put the pieces together.

"Excuse me, um, are you guys, like, Trump supporters?" I asked. I couldn't help myself.

The woman swiveled in her chair, giving me her attention.

"Fuck that motherfucker!" Her fists clenched as she exploded like a firework.

"So, you're not anti-gay?" I asked carefully.

"No! My daughter is gay, and I fully support her. And, honey . . . you shouldn't sleep outside. The KKK is very active out here." She took a sip from her mug and sank back into her chair.

The door swung open. "What a nice tent . . . you got there,"

Connor said. His energy was different from when I had gotten in his car a while ago. His wife got up and walked to the medicine cabinet, swallowed two pills, then put her eye cover on and earplugs in and retreated to the bed beside her desk. She was like a blinking baby doll, down as soon as she went horizontal.

It was just Connor and me.

In his left hand, he clutched a beer bottle. His eyes crept upon my face. I tried to ignore the groans coming from his mouth. He drooled over me like I were a perfect piece of medium-rare steak, the char too irresistible. The door was closed, and no lights illuminated the dark hall.

He mumbled under his breath. I had no idea what to expect from him. My Garmin rested in my right hand; in my left, the palm-sized blade of my pocketknife. *Let's go, motherfucker.*

I sat stiff, pretending to be on my phone, while Connor steamed beside me.

"Hey! Are you even listening to me?"

When I didn't respond, he exploded. "YOU ARE GOING TO LOOK ME IN THE EYE WHEN I TALK TO YOU! IN THIS HOUSE, YOU WILL LOOK ME IN MY GODDAMN EYES AND NOWHERE ELSE. Now, are you going to fucking sleep outside, or are you going to sleep on the couch? Because if you sleep on the couch, I am going to sleep right by you."

There wasn't time to think. I jumped to my feet and ran down the hall, pounding on Sage's door with heavy fists.

"Can I help you?" came the voice from inside.

"Yes, you can help me, please!" I yelled desperately, not daring to look back. "That man is yelling at me. I *do not* feel safe out there. I cannot stay here. I need to go back to the trail now. Please take me back."

The door opened. Sage looked unamused. "Oh, Connor, fuck him. Okay, okay, come in. You can stay in my room."

The energy in her room was creepy, eerie, and unnaturally silent. Sage sat me on her bed, where I remained stiff, my jaw clenched, jumping at the rustling outside the closed door. Connor's fists banged on the door, a coyote on the prowl, as tears streamed down my face. *This is it*, I said to myself. This was the point where the drunk angry white man went and got his gun, ready to take me out. I'd seen this in the movies so many times, except this wasn't a movie, and there were real-life consequences. How had I gotten myself here?

"I'll take care of him, just stay here," Sage reassured me. Then she rushed out of the room like a mama bear, charging Connor at full speed as I remained frozen in fear, barely able to watch, a cub hiding in her den.

"FUCK YOU, CONNOR! GET THE FUCK OUT OF HERE RIGHT NOW! Go to your room! Fucking don't come out, you son of a bitch!"

She came back in and slammed the door. "You okay?" she asked.

"Yes, thank you so much. Can I go back to the trail? I'm fucking scared. Why do you tolerate this man in your house? What about your mom?" My mouth couldn't be stopped. Forget mountains, bad weather, jagged rocks, or bears—this was the scariest event I'd ever faced on trail.

Sage sighed. "We . . . we need the money. We can't survive . . .

we can't survive without his money. I know it sounds stupid, but we try to ignore him. He's a fucking drunk, a bad man. He's not my father. . . ." Her voice trailed off.

I looked out of the window. Climbing out was an option, but I didn't do that. I couldn't help but pity them for having to live with a violent monster, a two-faced drunk. Everything made sense now.

"I can take you back to the trail first thing in the morning before Connor wakes up, but right now it's dark, and he's still up. It would be much safer in the morning. You can sleep on my bed, and I'll take the floor."

"Are you sure?" I was surprised by such an act of kindness.

"Yes, you've been through a lot. I'm so sorry that you had to go through all of this. It's the least I can do. Please, wake up at six a.m."

"Okay, sure. I'll break down my tent in the morning, too. Thank you so much."

She grabbed an air mattress from under the bed, blew it up, and put a white sheet over it. The lights went out, and I lay on my back. I snuggled into the comforter, Pepper's bed my safe place, my haven for the night. The events of the past few hours played in my mind. I was still here. I had made it, right?

I learned a valuable lesson that day while kicking myself in the ass for being stupid enough to go to this white man's house. I had been too comfortable accepting help from others. I'd let my guard down, a move that could have gotten me killed. Embracing hitching culture for the first time taught me that I couldn't do what white thru-hikers could do. Statements like "Just hitch" or "It's just an easy hitch" from white thru-hikers were spoken with privilege. The privilege of having white skin meant not having to consider how Black people were treated. It meant not having to worry about the KKK, being lynched, or being lured into the house of a racist man. It meant not understanding why a Black lesbian, a triple minority, would be afraid of hitching in white and well-known conservative towns, where racism was abundant and accepted as normal. My new normal was distrust and skepticism, questioning the intentions of anyone who offered help.

The next day, I woke up bright and early. After breaking down and packing up my tent, I noticed one alert on my Garmin. I clicked on it and read the message.

I am so sorry that I couldn't get to you last night. I had to respond to an accident in front of the store. Do you still need a ride? It's the shuttle driver.

I erased the message, grabbed my gear, and closed the door. There was only one place for me to go—the Appalachian Trail.

8

TAZEWELL, VIRGINIA

Thirty grueling miles later, crawling on my hands and knees, I
found myself at a road, ready to spend the night at the hostel
in Tazewell, Virginia. I called for the hostel shuttle and waited for
the sweet moment that my firm butt would bury itself in that car
seat. Anything soft was a relief from standing and walking, and I
was headed for a warm bunk and a hot breakfast.

The AT had groomed me well, but I almost forgot one of the most
important lessons she'd taught me: expect the unexpected. A pickup
truck pulled up. Inside, a middle-aged white man, wearing the
infamous Trump 2020 baseball cap.

Flashes of Connor cycled through my brain. *Should I stay or should
I go?* Though his demeanor was warm, once again, I felt like I was

in the wrong place, as if the comfort of being safely shuttled from one place to another was only reserved for white people. Yet after the past few days of tackling mountains with my head bent against the wind, the rain lashing at me, I was ready to give in. And so I did. He wasn't a stranger like Connor, I told myself, but just the hostel owner. This would not end the same way. I wouldn't allow it.

He opened the door and put my pack in the back seat, my comfort item gone, riding in the back seat behind me. Escape would be inconvenient. I surrendered and buckled down for the ride.

"You're Dragonsky, right? I think I follow you on Instagram."

What the actual fuck? How can you follow me on Instagram, knowing what I stand for, and then wear that hat? How does that even work, bro?

"Oh cool, thanks." I cringed with a smile. *Just play the game.*

He paused. His mouth could have stayed shut. Nothing more needed to be said.

"You know, you're much prettier in person than online."

"Thanks," I said, choosing the path of least resistance.

We pulled up to the hostel, a wide sturdy building lined with narrow white windows. Inside, I got the grand tour and was shown to a rustic bunk room. Usually I preferred the privacy and familiarity of my tent, but this was one of the cleaner hostels. Six bunks lined the wall, all empty except a single lower one. I chose the one closest to the door. Toilet location always dictated my choice of indoor hostel bunk. Hiker bladder is real. Every twenty minutes my bladder filled to its brim, nearly bursting out of my stomach. My brain associated nature with the toilet, subconsciously. There is no need to hold urine in its elastic sack when grass and rocks are plentiful. I was a wild animal now, the potty training I received as a child essential in civilization, but in nature the rules of the matrix don't apply. The forest is one giant toilet.

Satisfied with my accommodations, I settled in and wandered through the back door. Cows grazed on the small farm as the mountains peered from behind. A porch swing rocked in the wind, leaving me pondering if I should accept its invitation or explore the rest of the hostel. Before I could decide, the hostel owner's face appeared.

"You have a fan club coming in." He sighed, as if he was exhausted.

The peace was shattered with screams of delight.

"Dragonsky!" Three Black children tumbled into view, their eyes on fire.

It was the family from the Damascus diner. The trail had provided. Our paths had been meant to cross.

"Hey!" I yelled back.

They weren't the only surprise. Two other friends I'd met on the trail, Chai and Mocha, had booked a room at the hostel for the night. Since setting off in February, I'd seen Chai and Mocha several times as we had a similar pace, averaging about eight to eleven miles a day, not worrying about distance. At hostels, we slackpacked together, which is when someone takes your stuff for the day as you complete a section, usually between two roads, taking the burden off your back during intense climbs. We spent much of our time around the cozy fire, reminiscing about the difficulties and triumphs on the mountains. Whenever I seemed to be down in the dumps, that pair of lovebirds flew by to lift my spirits.

At the sight of them along with this little hiking family, all the discomfort I had felt from the hostel owner lifted like a fog cloud drifting away from the crown of a mountain. Never before had I felt so safe. We were all people of color under the roof of a Trump supporter. Had I finally found my trail family—my tramily?

With this reassurance, I made the choice to approach the family. *Now is my chance.*

"Hey, my name is Dragonsky, as you already know, but it's nice to formally meet you. What are y'all's names?"

My eyes met those of the mother. She had a softness in her voice, calm enough to soothe anyone. We were both short, but she was slightly taller than I. Her brown hair was frayed like shredded wires.

"Hi, I'm Turtle. It's nice to meet you," she said. "I'll let the girls introduce themselves."

"I'm Grumpy Cat," said the tallest girl, who looked to be the oldest.

The second girl, who had chimed in, "I'm Jumprope, and this is Bobo!"

Bobo, the youngest, peered timidly around her mother, her clothes a kaleidoscope of cotton-candy colors. She watched as the other girls laughed and talked to me, her nut-brown eyes inspecting me closely. She was shy around newcomers, unlike Jumprope, who was chatty. Layers of long locs branched out like elephant ears down to Jumprope's shoulders. Questions and curiosity about the world flowed from her lips, and I adored her for it. She reminded me of what I was like as a nine-year-old girl—hungry for knowledge. Grumpy Cat still had a few years on her to bloom, but she was coming into her prime. Her younger sisters appeared to be more of an annoyance to her than anything. She seemed sick of their shit, but that was to be expected for a thirteen-year-old.

We agreed to set off on the AT together the next day, our bodies gravitating toward one another's like long-lost family members at a reunion. Through the swirl of excitement came the sound of my aunt's voice, carried in the soft wind. Clarity came to me. Family wasn't always blood, and blood wasn't always thicker than water. Sometimes family was chosen, and Turtle, Grumpy Cat, Jumprope, and Bobo were just that. This family was choosing me to be a part of their hike, through thick and thin. Someone wanted me in my raw form, stinking, hyper, and goofy. I realized I had a family born of pure love, and how could I not love that? After weeks of solo hiking, my soul was anchored to this new reality, and I didn't want the bond to dissolve.

I was not a huge fan of kids in general, but these girls were special. Their giggles, their smiles, and the way they bounced down the trail became my new normal over the next few days. With pencil legs that I thought could snap at any minute, the girls were the true badasses of the trail. They lifted their heads, eyes closed in glory, knees shaking. At first I had worried about whether they were too young to thru-hike the AT, too small to surmount its obstacles, but they quickly reminded me that children are the hardiest, most resilient, and most flexible of us all—they couldn't be stopped. In their eyes I saw the light of the world, and in mine, a reflection of theirs. Finding them and knowing we shared similar experiences brought our hearts closer. I was no longer facing the cruel realities of racism on trail alone. We were a force, together. It was then that

I realized how much of a role model I could be for them, and for Black girls around the world. Crowned like royalty, we walked like Black queens, taking up space in a place that was never meant for us.

Most people didn't want to confront race on the trail. It was a sloth in the room, a sluggish topic not worthy of attention in a place that was 99.9 percent white. The truth was we were all hiking the same trail. I wanted that to matter most, and to be treated no differently than anyone else—and 95 percent of the time, that was what happened. I was accepted by other hikers, and many respected me for who I was. But still, in certain towns and a few hostels, I was made aware of my Blackness. It amazed me how bold white people were when it came to being racist right in Black people's faces. Nice or not, that hostel owner had still worn that hat. Children were not stupid; they knew what that hat represented. As a Black woman, I had been taught to be peaceful with white people while enduring slurs, gut-wrenching stares, and uncomfortable conversations. On Guthooks, hikers left comments about the types of hostels on the Appalachian Trail where owners used the word *nigger* and bore their flags like they would six-point buck antlers. White hikers continued to patronize these hostels while leaving good reviews, their silence hurting people of color.

Turtle and I connected over the racism the kids and I had experienced on the trail. A white woman, Turtle had adopted her three girls. She strongly advocated for them while being aware that she had privileges they would never have. She shared with me her hardships while raising Black girls and how white people tried to touch their hair and ask her ignorant questions. Although she climbed mountains every day on the trail, I knew the mountains she had to climb for her girls were insurmountable. Black girls in America are forced to face the realities of racism from the time they are born. In school, Black girls endure harsher discipline than their white counterparts and are body-slammed, handcuffed, and reported for any suspicious behavior that is deemed not age appropriate. Black girls are subjected to the same stereotypes that Black women are subjected to and fall victim to police killings with no justice. We are told we are not enough.

But we are enough, and we always will be. In division, we find unity, and in unity, I found a tramily. All that I had dreamed of had come true at a hostel in East Bumblefuck, Virginia.

Turtle was slow and steady, providing us countless opportunities to bond and explore the trail like the little girls we were. Nature was one big playground, and age didn't matter. Decaying trees became seesaws, mud puddles deep abysses of gunk to smear on the face and paint the earth with. I admired Turtle's strength to hike with three children, and I admired the love for nature she had instilled in them. With them, hiking wasn't about the destination but about immersion. Foraging for wild ramps, teaching the kids how to start and kindle a fire, and singing Disney songs were some of our favorite activities during the next two hundred miles that we spent together, on and off. The constant sounds of the siblings arguing and singing the lyrics to *Hamilton* filled me with a deep sense of contentment. The closest I had ever come to this feeling was when I was with my Aunt Barbara, during the times I lived with her and Uncle Amos in Manchester. I could hear the Christmas bells jingling, the sweet tune of the musical lights wrapped around the tree as the children chased each other in the backyard.

But like with all other things I'd experienced in my life, this bubble of safety and comfort didn't last. One morning, I decided I needed to stay behind to take a break. I had always been a slow hiker, and I knew, eventually, that I wouldn't be able to match their pace. We said goodbye casually and hugged, and I gave the girls my word that I would try to catch up.

As I watched them vanish into the green abyss, a sinking feeling suddenly came over me. I choked on my tears. What had I done? Why had I let them go? Had I lost them, forever?

That night I found myself at a hostel called Angels Rest, a popular spot for carnivores and partygoers. Angels Rest was loaded with tents strewn all over the yard because the bunks inside were booked out. I was hanging out with a few hikers around my age, engaging in pleasant conversation, trying to flush the image of Turtle and the girls from my mind. How many miles had they covered? How many would I have to do to catch up with them? As I fumbled with my thoughts, I hardly noticed when two older white men approached our table. I smiled and gave them a gentle hello, but what I received in return disturbed me.

"May I ask you something?" one of them said out of the blue. "I heard ya talking about white people and racists. I got family that fought in the Union Army, so why am I called that? I ain't no different from you. I don't see color, so I shouldn't be called a racist."

"If you think you don't see color, that's a problem right there," I said.

But he kept going. "I haven't done nothing to Black people."

"How do you know they're Black people if you don't see color?"

"Just because I want to fly the Confederate flag doesn't mean—"

I lost my cool, the façade I was constantly forced to keep up around people like this. "Hey. Shut the fuck up. I am not the spokesperson for all Black people."

"But I just want to know why—"

"Get. The. Fuck. Out. Of. My. Space."

As the men grudgingly left, I sensed a gentle presence behind me. It was the white woman who worked at the hostel, Hot Tamale.

"Hey. You did a great job defending yourself, even when you shouldn't have had to."

"Thanks."

"Growing up in Savannah, all I knew were Black people, and they were the kindest to me. Y'all go through so much, and this shit just gets to me. I think those men need to leave the space."

"I agree," I said, relieved. Angels Rest was living up to its name: Here was an angel looking out for me, and she was a fireball. Deep down, I was taken aback by this act of kindness and protection. Here in front of me was a true ally who refused to remain silent and let the carnage continue. I had already seen the kindness of other heroes and angels on the trail, offering water and sharing food with those who didn't have any, and I had done the same. I had seen hikers whose companions had gotten injured and who never left their side, accompanying them back to the nearest road to get into town. Kindness on the trail manifested itself in a variety of ways, and here it had saved me once again.

After the traumatic event, I wanted nothing more than to be with my tramily. I knew we were a force when we were together, but when we were separated, trouble always seemed to find me, and I battled hostile environments and people just to try to catch up with them again. I didn't want to be a single, isolated tree, leaving myself vulnerable to exposure. I wanted to be within the cluster of trees because I knew that if we stuck together, we could weather any storm.

There was another reason why I hadn't been able to keep up with Turtle and the girls. On the trail, heartbreak had come to me like a strike of lightning. I had not planned for it. There was nowhere to hide or run. I had believed that nature would heal all wounds. But healing this broken heart of mine was not meant to be.

I had always said I would never fall in love. Until I did, the possibility had never entered my mind. The deep narrative of my subconscious told me I wasn't good enough, at least not for love. My past relationships were toxic, reflecting the memories of my childhood. My partners were the broken pieces of myself that I was trying to heal, abuse was common, and true love was rare. I'd given up after my last relationship, vowing that I would never be trapped in such a dangerous situation again.

But then in December 2020 I fell in love with Zuri, just as I was falling in love with the Appalachian Trail. Our love was a wildfire, its path of destruction only beginning to show once the smoke had settled.

The chaos of our relationship was of our own making. I'd met

Zuri at a mutual friend's house while playing Uno. Our paths had crossed once before at a friend's birthday party, but in the presence of Zuri's then-girlfriend, I became reserved. Meeting a second time was the work of the spiritual realm, we decided, and on my way out the door, she asked me for my phone number. Thinking that it would just be a good fuck, I took it, and she came over two days later, knocking on my door with a savory quiche in her hand as if instinctively knowing that food was my love language. We ate hastily and made our way into my bedroom, taking turns playing *Tony Hawk's Pro Skater* on my PS4 and learning more about each other. We both loved gospel music, dancing, and traveling. We talked about the corruption of capitalism and our desire to live in Canada. I saw the sunlight in her eyes, and I stared even though I knew it would burn or blind me.

"Stop looking at me like that," she said one day.

"Like what?"

"You know what. That look you're giving me." She rolled her eyes. Then she said, "Is it okay if I touch you?"

Her lips stroked the edge of mine, delicately, like butterfly wings, while my heart fluttered in my chest.

"Yes, but just one thing: Don't fall in love with me," I said.

Our clothes came off, and she took me into her for hours.

Our attraction was like rock climbing. As if she were the climber and I the belayer, keeping her from tumbling down, our eyes communicating the thoughts we dared not speak. Tethered to each other, we became hesitant to let go, but she and I both knew she had to eventually come down. That evening I let her spend the night, and we barely slept. We talked until the morning birds called, touching on the topic of her six-year-old relationship.

"My girlfriend is moving to Atlanta, and we agreed to have an open sexual relationship as long as there aren't any feelings involved. She knows I am interested in you. The first time we met at the party, I whispered to her about how cute you are."

Reassured by Zuri that I wasn't a homewrecker and that she wasn't cheating on her girlfriend, a switch flipped in my brain.

Zuri came over the next day, and the next day, and the next. For the whole month of January 2021, we spent every hour of each day together, fucking, talking, and playing in the snow. She majored in music, played the drums, guitar, and piano, and aspired to start her own band someday. She loved to read poems from a small pink book she carried around like the Bible. Her car, a red Toyota, was named Pizza. Zuri was a tulip, and I the hummingbird sipping up every last drop of her nectar. I'd never tasted anything so heady, and I was afraid I would soon be too drunk to see clearly.

The day I left for the AT, just two months after we'd met, we fucked and then cried in each other's arms, expecting our friendship to end. We'd already fought many times over the feelings we'd concealed for each other, swearing it would be the best decision to break it off, only to find ourselves dancing back to each other. This push and pull continued for months while I was on the trail; trying to break the spell only made the magic stronger.

It was now June 2021, and I had just been told that there was a new girl she'd met back home. They were fucking. Suddenly I was choking, struggling to breathe. I was sentenced to a new solitary confinement, the trees my bars holding me in, tying me down to a trail I had committed to doing while Zuri carried on elsewhere. My brain was a desperate prisoner, begging the guard to release me. She had been an unexpected distraction, one I had sought to cast away before even stepping foot on the trail, yet her ghost still lingered here.

Most days on the trail, I felt like I owned the place. This was my home, the great wilderness where I belonged. But now I was glued to my tent some mornings, sobbing and asking myself why no one could love me for me. I thought incessantly about her to the point that I compromised my progress, only able to hike two miles a day. Zuri was part of the reason I fell behind the ones who truly loved me, Turtle and the girls.

Without my tramily, the Virginia Blues started to creep up on me like a vine of greenbrier, its thorns piecing my side. I dreamed of them. Again and again and again. The trail demanded that I keep pushing on alone; it was the only possibility of reuniting with them. Just like what much of the trauma in my life had taught me, going forward was the only way. Based on texts I received from Turtle, they were at least a week ahead, forcing me to pick up my pace and daily mileage. Averaging eight to ten miles a day was simply not sufficient, and I pushed to fifteen to try to catch up with them. But each day I slipped behind even farther, a new challenge arose, or my past caught up with me.

9

FULL MOON

By the young age of twelve years old, I was already infected. I raged, an ailment that blinded my judgment and stole every drop of my energy. A rage fueled by a radioactive pit of energy that could not be measured or contained. I began to act out. There were times I was Dr. Jekyll, but other times I was Mrs. Hyde.

"She can be sweet sometimes," my aunt would say. That statement was also a favorite line of my cousin Nikki. As a natural-born snitch, Nikki was always snooping through my diaries and spilling the goods or listening in on my phone calls. She would reiterate this "sometimes sweet" description to other people, which really melted my ice cream.

Who are you to tell them that? You're a part of the problem. You pick up the line, listen to my phone calls, and burn me. You do NOT have the right to tell anyone how I am.

She was such a hypocrite, but I was always the bad guy. People at church began to hear about my increasingly bad behavior. Let me get this straight: It was okay to tell others about how bad I was acting out but not okay to talk about the molestation and trauma I had endured? It was a double standard, and I called bullshit.

My anger manifested through my mouth. Talking back and not giving a shit was what I did best, especially when I hit puberty. Eighth grade through sophomore year of high school, my behavior was out of control. I'd get into it with Aunt Barbara.

"You can't tell me what to do. I'm a preteen! I'm a teenager!"

She would stand there shocked and hurt, but most of all, she was disappointed. This tiny human she had saved from the jungle had grown up and was becoming a monster. Phones, stuffed animals, and even shoes became projectiles targeted not just at my aunt but also at Nikki. After all the years of being tormented by the sexual assault, plus Nikki's treatment of me, I had had it. Nikki was my aunt's second-born daughter and took the role of the "baby" very seriously. Leave it to younger sisters to always get jealous if anyone threatens that special treatment. The thing is, she had over ten years on me, so she'd had the privilege of watching me grow up. I remembered she used to take me places with her when I was just a tiny nugget. I would sit in the passenger seat and criticize her for smoking cigarettes.

"Can you please stop smoking? I don't want you to die!" I must have looked at her with the most charming puppy-dog eyes she had ever seen, because she tossed the whole pack right out the damn window. Of course, my pleas would eventually be ignored, but regardless of the physical fights, taunts, gross jealousy, and the days I wanted to kill her, I still looked up to her. I loved her.

But gone were the days of being a little girl. I was going through puberty and slowly growing into a woman. Nikki and I were constantly at it tooth and nail, but a lot of it started with her; I just sought to finish the job. I never could, though, because she was a heavyset woman with the strength of an ox. My aunt would tell her to leave me alone, but my uncle was indifferent to Nikki's treatment of me. Uncle Amos was Aunt Barbara's keeper, and for me to disrespect his wife with my antics was unacceptable to him.

My uncle and I had had a great relationship when I was a child, but as I entered my teen years, I'm pretty sure he couldn't stand my ass. *Sapsucker* was his word of choice for me, and I didn't have a single clue what that meant. I was like a Pavlovian dog: When he said that word, something in my brain went, *Okay, this word means bad things are to come.* If I was doing something bad, that meant I deserved to be called a sapsucker and possibly chased around the house or told I was going to get thrown over the fence. Sometimes it felt as though he was being mean just to be mean, and I would run and hide behind Aunt Barbara.

"Leave that baby alone please, Amos!" she would yell. Even when I was bad, her defense of me spoke multitudes about her character. Did he leave me alone? Sometimes. Did I deserve it? Looking back, no kid deserves to be called names, but he knew no better. Aunt Barbara's approach was different, and when she reached her limit, she gave me back to my mother and grandmother. Anytime I was sent back, I sobbed like someone had taken my puppy. (Someone had already done so—Tigger, the Shih Tzu Aunt Barbara had gotten for me in elementary school, was stolen from their front yard one day, which broke my heart.) I'd promise that I would be a good girl, but we all knew that was way beyond me.

It wasn't that I wasn't trying. It was that I was troubled. I was screaming for help—inside and out loud.

Resentment grew when I was sent back to live with my mother. I hated her. I was taught never to feel or express hatred, as it was ungodly. But I couldn't help it. My stomach curdled when I saw her. A sour and thick substance with foul, chunky mush. I thought that if only my body could be cut open and some of the more traumatic events removed, then maybe my mother and I could be casual.

I remained respectful but distant from my mother while I continued to disrespect my aunt. Power took on an entirely new meaning; it was not to be taken from me. Nothing could be taken from me, I promised myself, not food, clothes, shelter, not even Six Flags tickets. At least not without a fight—which almost always ended in my loss.

One day in particular, I completely lost my marbles.

I was staying with my aunt at the time. I had just come home from hanging out with the kids next door on a Saturday evening. Peace and quiet filled the little house with the purple shutters, but war was waging within me. I wasn't allowed to watch *Pokémon*, *Yu-Gi-Oh*, or *Digimon* because the church deemed it "demonic material." That's what the Christian church loved to do: take, take, and take some more. But something was brewing within me. I sat down on the couch and turned the TV on to *Yu-Gi-Oh*. No sooner had I watched a few minutes than my aunt came home, catching me engaging in the so-called "demonic activity." She grabbed the remote from me. Frustrated, I lost my temper.

"Why? It's not fair what the church says!"

Talking back only escalated the situation, and my aunt got a leather belt out.

No one is going to hit me. I've been hit enough.

We were like dogs tugging back and forth on a rope—until one of us gave. Aunt Barbara's knees hit the ground. Tears welled up in her eyes. Withered, exhausted, and physically incapacitated, there was nothing more left that she could do.

I froze. What had I done? I loved my Aunt Barbara, and she had been recently diagnosed with kidney disease and was put on dialysis every single day. I knew she was sick, but it didn't stop me from being disrespectful. I also didn't fully grasp her diagnosis and what that meant for her; I just knew that she went away during the day, and they filtered her blood so it could be clean. Her disease purged her of the strength she once had, as her body needed every breath and heartbeat to fight for her. Kidney disease stole from her kidneys the ability to filter out toxins, and she was limited in the amount of fluids she could drink. She only drank water, and when she was getting to the end of her day's rations, she converted to chewing on ice cubes. Diabetes also hopped on board, causing a war I wouldn't wish on my worst enemy. Blue to black, her skin tissue eroded like a beach that was hit with a storm. Her toes suffered the worst. She eventually lost one; amputation was the only option. Glaucoma also fogged over one of her eyes. Her ship was in distress, slowly going from a glorious, formidable vessel to a wearied kayak with eroded oars.

Harrowing as it was, her anchors stayed put in the sand below. Most of all, she still had heart, and her spirit never dimmed. Even as my behavioral issues piled up like bricks.

What I didn't know then but do now is that it is normal for a child to be hypersexual following sexual trauma. Many victims of sexual abuse become either hypersexual or asexual. In his book *Resurrection After Rape*, Matt Atkinson breaks down this behavior even further. The sexual actions of survivors are a result of their inner pain, and it is their inner hurt, not their personal worth, that drives the cycle. These actions are a sign of despair that cannot be expressed in words and can only be brought to light through certain behaviors. For survivors, sex may have lost its value, or they may be trying to gain a false sense of control after feeling helpless and afraid. They may believe giving means they will not be hurt again. Many reconnect to the meaninglessness and humiliation of the abuse through meaningless and humiliating sex in an effort to give their grief an opportunity to finally be expressed.

I wanted and needed my power back. Instead I was labeled a slut, a whore, and promiscuous. No one understood my pain, not even me. As I blossomed into adulthood, my chest filled to a full C cup, my hips widened, and my hormones went bonkers. I had already started my period in fifth grade, and it felt like I was becoming a woman faster than my brain could keep up. Grown men stared at me like I was a piece of New York strip steak, which only made me feel like a sex object. The catcalling started. Almost every thought I had was about sex, and I felt that I needed to have sex to feel loved, to feel heard, and to feel wanted. By the time I was fourteen, any boy who came my way I fucked; it didn't matter that I didn't like them. I actually found the sex repulsive.

I had known I was a lesbian since I started school, even though I did not know the word. Even my favorite cousin looked at me when I was seven and said, "You gonna be gay." In my diary, I wrote about women every day while I struggled with these thoughts. The first entry was dated the year 2001, when I was a fifth grader. I finished the entry with "Please don't let me be gay, oh god, I think I'm gay." In kindergarten I had an intense crush on a girl named Sarah, and I was always flattered when she shared her blocks with me. In elementary school, I had a crush on my music teacher, and in middle school I had a crush on one of my English teachers. As strange as it sounds, I also used to kiss my Ashanti posters. I was in love with her, swearing that I would meet her someday. Sunday mornings at church increasingly became a struggle as I developed crushes on a few singers, dancers, and family friends. It was bad enough that my aunt would ask, "Shilletha, are you gay? All you do is talk about these women from church all the—"

"No, not at all. I just really look up to them."

That was the biggest lie I ever told. Hesitation would provoke concerns, and I didn't want to cause issues or be disowned. After all, it was the early 2000s, and the way society viewed homosexuality was that "these people" weren't normal. Hate was in the air. "Don't

Ask, Don't Tell" was still the law of the land, within the military and outside. Running the risk of someone finding out you were a "deviant" meant potentially being booted out of the service. You could—and can still—lose out on a potential place to live if you were a homeless youth who identified as lesbian, gay, bisexual, transgender, and/or queer. Out in society, your very life could be on the line; those who were out of the closet were constantly called faggots and dykes.

As terrifying as everything was, nothing scared me more than the church. My church, like most in the Christian religion, opposed homosexuality and made every attempt to make that known. We were abominations who were deemed unnatural, and the pastors would use the Bible to justify their hate, though they missed the Biblical passages about eunuchs and David and Jonathan. They missed the part that went, "For God so loved the world that he gave his one and only Son, that whoever believes in him shall not perish but have eternal life." Instead, they focused on us. In Black families, many are not accepting, even to this day, especially Black men who feel emasculated and threatened by gay men and trans women in our communities. I couldn't let them know about me.

I thought that if I slept with men, my homosexual urges would go away. They never did; they only intensified and added another cement block on my chest, leading to a deep darkness that I couldn't tunnel out of. The walk-in closet in my aunt's room became a daily space for routine prayer, and a place to hide from myself. Prayer, I thought, good old-fashioned prayer could get these vile, immoral thoughts out of my head. I was a child of God, and God did not like gays like me. Every night I prayed the same prayer: "Dear God and Jesus, please don't let me be gay. Please take away these thoughts. I believe in your son Jesus Christ and that he died on the cross for my sins. Please forgive me for sinning—for lying, being mean, and especially being gay. I don't want these feelings. Please, God, take it away. In Jesus's name, amen."

For every prayer, there needed to be an accompanying action. You didn't just pray for God to make you lose weight while continuing to eat pizza and ice cream. My plan of action was to pray, sleep with men, date men, and act girly. What actually happened was that I prayed, fantasized about women while sleeping with men, continued to be boyish, and protested being put in dresses. I wet my hair when it was freshly pressed and refused to carry purses. It was a battle that couldn't be won.

There was nowhere to hide from myself. Like my mother used to say, "No matter where you move, go, or drive, just remember you still have to take Shilletha with you." I fought myself, and it took a toll on my mental health. My cutting intensified, thoughts of worthlessness prevailed, and the black hole of my anxiety swallowed me. Worst of all, every day felt like Halloween. I had to put on a costume at all times to go to church and school or be in front of my family.

The same friend who snitched me out for cutting the first time was also struggling with their sexual orientation. I knew Gina was a lesbian because we both gawked and drooled over our insanely hot Spanish teacher. We had no interest in learning Spanish; we just wanted to have an image in our minds so that we could go home later and have phone sex with each other over it. Beautiful teachers would stroll by, and we would stroll right up next to them. We both tried to talk it out of each other, stating that we were going to hell and would never see our loved ones again. I don't know if she dealt with any anxiety on top of it, but I know many in our community become paranoid, develop or have worsening anxiety, self-harm, and attempt or successfully complete ending our lives. Staying closeted and living in fear takes a toll. The sad truth is that LGBTQIA persons are more than twice as likely as heterosexual adults to experience a mental health condition. We are at a higher risk of suicide; in fact, we are five times more likely to attempt ending our lives in comparison with those who identify as cisgender heterosexuals.

To be a Black woman who is a lesbian with mental illness is a triple threat. The stigma is akin to being seen as a weak Black woman; I was succumbing to my mental state and failing to fight as hard as my ancestors had fought during slavery. I was seen as the crazy girl who needed to seek God for healing and was told that the source of the cutting was all in my head. Because, you know, "everyone has issues."

I was an abomination, forced to feel that I deserved the names and the humiliation of being called out in the classroom by a class-mate who said, "Shilletha, yeah, she's the biggest dyke ever," while everyone gasped and laughed. To be branded in society, and by those I loved, made trust impossible for me. To make things worse, when it seemed nothing else would work, Aunt Barbara resorted to wielding shame as a weapon. She began telling people whom I was close to at church and who had no idea how I acted at home about everything. They stopped doing nice things for me, even though all I needed was someone to care. I felt like I was marked with a neon *D* for deviant.

Struggling with my sexuality and mental health with a lack of a support system put too many apples in my basket. Inevitably, my behavior took a violent turn, and I exhibited the three infamous traits of a serial killer, also known as the Macdonald triad. Fire-setting, bed-wetting, and cruelty to animals were the criteria—and I met all three.

I peed in bed up until I was nine; I even had a few accidents in middle school, but by then I knew how to do the laundry. Fire became a flame I could tame, and watching it became a fascination, the glowing amber releasing black smoke into the air as I watched my teddy bears, paper, and plastic burn. Lastly, the cruelty to animals—something that I am not proud of. I liked to play with bugs and enjoyed drowning them in water or performing "thorax removal surgery," in which I took scissors, cut off the thoraxes, and waited for them to wake up to see how they would react. Insects were small talk, and my obsession turned to bigger animals like frogs. There were plenty around in the yard, and many of them I caught and released. But one day, one had to die. Why? I am not sure what compelled me to grab the scissors from the kitchen drawer and put holes in the frog like it was a pincushion. Its small heart still beat for a while after.

The frog meant nothing to me. Just another body, another piece of matter taking up space without purpose, folly, or fame. The heart was striving for life even outside the vessel that had encased it. That was the last animal I hurt. Such a vile and cruel act that was fueled by emptiness and a reflection of self.

My need for purpose, love, inclusion, and a mother was insatiable. There was a crack in my soul that could not be filled. I was a ghost who wandered through time and memories looking for the perfect vessel to possess that would allow for my growth, development, and peace of mind.

Belonging was the only thing I needed. I craved a warm hug and a mother's touch—anything. I hadn't asked to be born to a dysfunctional mother, so I decided to choose a new one. And the more mother figures I had, the more protected and wanted I felt.

It started at church with a few of my friends' mothers. I would hang out with my friends and see how their mothers treated them, and if it was acceptable behavior, I would hang out a bit more with my friends to get closer to their mothers. I looked for instructions for what to do next, where to go, and who to love.

I must have asked at least six women to be my mother throughout my young life, and each time I was rejected. These were my friends' parents, and I could not expect them to fit me in with their biological children.

I was a little girl struggling to understand why no one wanted me. I wanted to have a normal family, but what was normal anyway? The fear of abandonment bit at me like relentless mosquitos. My stomach rumbled as if it had been deprived of the food of love, my appetite insatiable. I had to find this food before death approached.

I knew I had love and support from Aunt Barbara, but there was always a need for more. She could have been enough, but I was blinded. I didn't realize she was my guardian, my aunt, and my mother all at once. Every day she poured a little more love into my glass, which I left untouched. The glass was nearly full, waiting for me, but one year later, before I could drink, it fell over.

10

WAXING GIBBOUS

Wednesday, January 17, 2007, started out like any other school day. I woke up around six a.m., got dressed, ate my cereal, and collected my lunch money from my aunt.

"Have a good day at school," she told me.

I was fifteen and a sophomore in high school. As I grabbed my backpack and headed out, she remained in bed, presumably waiting until it was time for dialysis. That day, the vocational school representative was coming to show us one of the alternate routes to a higher education, which were the trades. One of the programs instantaneously caught my interest: the Marine Academy of Technology and Environmental Sciences. The program was built for those who were interested in pursuing a career in the STEM field and would prepare students for science, math, and technology courses upon entering college. I loved that the classes were hands-on and dealt with aquatic science because I aspired to be a marine biologist at the time. With great enthusiasm I took one of the brochures that the representative handed out to eager students looking for a way out of their mundane routines.

I got home that afternoon to an unusual sight. White, green, and silver cars were arranged in the driveway of my house with the purple shutters as if they were sardines stuffed into a can.

Is it a party? Is there a surprise waiting for my aunt when she gets home? So many damn cars. Some familiar, some unknown.

As I walked through the door, vocational school papers in hand, I flashed a quick smile at the faces around me. I knew those faces. I knew those people. They were family, friends. But they weren't smiling back.

Why aren't they smiling? Energy flows in a field that most cannot detect. It flowed magnetically from the crown of my forehead directly into the deepest pit of my stomach. Suddenly everything was so heavy, as if all the seven seas had submerged me, weights bound to my ankles. Something wasn't right.

I made my way to my aunt's room. Aunt Barbara was missing. My eyes immediately darted to my uncle, who was sitting in the rocking chair. Hands that were once so strong were now fragile and idle. He turned to me and uttered the words that I will never forget.

"She's gone."

"Who's gone? What—what do you mean *gone*?!"

My hands began to tremble. Nothing in my fifteen years of life on this planet could have prepared me for what came next.

"Your Aunt Barbara . . . she's gone."

In an instant, the world came to an abrupt stop. The papers fell softly to the ground, and a chilling scream pierced the silence in the house. I collapsed to the ground as though a bullet had struck my heart. Everyone gathered around me and tried to help me stand up, but I was a boulder.

I found out that she had gone to dialysis that day, and when they called her name to receive treatment, she stood up, had a heart attack, and died. The medical professionals tried to revive her, but there was nothing anyone could do. The worst part was that the hospital was right across the street.

I pictured my aunt sitting in the pink cushioned chair in the waiting room of the dialysis center, surrounded by its white walls and inspirational pictures of nature and landscapes composed of farms and rolling hills. I saw her nodding her head to "How Great Is Our God," a song that my church played religiously and that she loved.

She sang that song like Mariah Carey in her prime. I imagined music playing inside her head, giving her the comfort and peace to make it through another trying day of dialysis. Little did she know that moments later she would be singing with the angels, greeted by her mother, who would tell her it was okay to let go, that she was home now. I thought about the terrifying moments we had had over the past few months, when I would be engaging her in conversation one minute and the next she would be slumped back on the couch, eyes rolled to the back of her head, unresponsive.

Multiple times I had taken her for dead as I watched this occur, but each time she came back.

I lay down on the carpet right beside my aunt's bed. Months before, I'd had a dream that I now knew was a vision, predicting this as clear as day. The vision was of me coming home from school to friends and family members who had shown up at the house. Then, suddenly, I teleported to our church in North Carolina and was standing in front of a rose-tinted casket containing the body of my aunt. The church was full, and soft gospel music filled the atmosphere. I had already seen the flowers and even smelled the church months before she actually died.

At the time, this "dream" had scared the living shit out of me, and I ran to my aunt. She was standing between the sink and the stove cooking some pork chops, lima beans, and macaroni and cheese.

"Aunt Barbara, um . . . I had a dream you were going to die, and it scared me."

"It's probably going to happen soon," she responded coolly. I didn't know how to react and just laughed it off.

As I wallowed in the fresh waves of grief, another unsettling memory came rushing back to me. I played junior varsity basketball at the time and our team even made it to states, but most of those victories were never witnessed by Aunt Barbara, who was usually at dialysis or feeling too under the weather to attend. However, the Tuesday before she died, she sat at my home game and cheered for me. When we went home right after the game, my aunt wanted to see me in her room just to talk. We had done this many times throughout my childhood, just to hang out and watch *The Lion King 2: Simba's Pride*, sing along to *The Cheetah Girls*, or paint our nails together, but something was different this time. I sat on the carpet and looked into my aunt's eyes. Hues both black and blue circled her left eye in a bull's-eye ring. Her skin was now shriveled and begging for water, even though her hair remained as curly as it had always been. I sat with my blue-and-gold basketball jersey embroidered with the number twelve, ears ready.

She began. "One day, Shilletha, I am not going to be here, and I need you to know that it will be okay. There will be people in this life to lead you on your way. Just because I die doesn't mean the world ends. I want you to take care of yourself. I am sick because when I was your age, I ate a bunch of junk and did not take care of my body. I do not want you to end up like me. Go to college and do everything you set out to do. You mustn't stop following your dreams and being what you want to be. It will all be okay."

I listened, at a loss for words. *Why? Why is she telling me this now? Where is this coming from?*

I tuned her message out because it gave me chills. My brain could not process her words, and I shrugged it off. *Yeah, right*, I said to myself.

Her message had meant nothing to me that Tuesday night. But now she was gone, and I was awake to my new reality. I knew I would carry those words with me for the rest of my life.

The family planned a funeral in North Carolina, which had become a place of mourning for me. I had already attended about ten funerals of relatives over the past five years, including that of my grandmother, Momma Nan. But this one would throw my whole world upside down. We weren't even supposed to have a service in North Carolina because my aunt had disclosed to me prior that she wanted to be buried in New Jersey, the magnificent state she called home, where the opalescent yellow American goldfinches fed in the orchards; where seemingly timid common blue violets emerged into the sunlight on fields that receded into the depths of the pine barrens; where snow-covered beaches in the dead of winter were battered by the pounding of waves; where the muffled sounds of humans could be heard striking each other with snowballs. Honoring her wish was my desire, but when I brought it up to my uncle, he refused to listen. I was just a kid, after all.

Brothers, sisters, cousins, friends, church members, and others came from near and far. Black is usually the color for such an occasion, but we decided to choose another: white, to represent rebirth and life during this celebration of her life. Death had no victory here. Yet *devastation* was the only word I knew to describe the looks on everyone's faces. Tears could not be concealed and flowed like mother's milk. Even the sky cried. "A Song for Mama" by Boys II Men, a song I had never heard prior to my aunt's death, became the anthem of her funeral. The song was supposed to be sung by a family friend, but grief devoured her and she could not continue. My grief surged with every breath I took. As if I were climbing a huge mountain, the higher I went, the less air I had to breathe. Crying in front of people was an embarrassment to me, but I had never experienced grief like this before. I clutched the obituary and sobbed.

When it was time, I made my way up to Aunt Barbara. Two by two, we walked like military personnel, until the march could no longer continue. I looked down on my aunt, who appeared to be in a peaceful slumber. A few sparkles of glitter were on her face. She had always been a star. She always shone.

Here lay my mother. The mother who had taught me wrong from right, the one who picked me up while I was sick and carried me, the one who believed in me. She had always been that light for me, and now that light was gone. I hadn't been by her side when she died to tell her it would be okay, but by her casket, I got the chance to tell her that I loved her one last time.

I had prepared a piece to read at her funeral. Public speaking was not my thing at all, and quite frankly, I thought it would be a shit show. But I maintained my composure and delivered my first speech—a final farewell.

"First and foremost, I want to dedicate this to my Aunt Barbara for always being there, raising me, and putting up with me. I love you, and you know that because I told you before I went to bed that night. For you are only sleeping. I'll see you again when my time comes. 'For we know that when this tent we live in now is taken down . . . when we die and leave these bodies . . . we will have wonderful new bodies in heaven, homes that will be ours forevermore, made for us by God himself and not by human hands.' Two Corinthians, chapter five, verse one. To be absent from the body is to be present with the Lord. I know you are watching over me, and I'm going to make you proud. You live in my heart forever."

Then I recited a poem I had written the day she died, titled "Why."

2007 I thought it was a happy New Year
But now I'm sitting here crying out tears
Back when I was a baby
I know I drove my aunt crazy
I cried and cried
I know she loves me she really tried
I remember those days she would sing to me
And she wanted to see when I grew up what I would be
She won't even have that chance in the flesh
'Cause she breathed her last breath
It's over and I feel so alone
This is a sadness I've never known
She said she would go to my graduation and watch me get married
But now look at the burden I'm carrying
I need my close friends and my family
Most of all I need someone to believe in me
God has her under his wings
With all the angels and other things
She raised me and saved my life
And no way could I pay for that price
I have a hole in my heart that no one can replace
Because no one will take her place
Every time I try so hard not to cry
But all I want to know is why?

Nikki—my aunt's own daughter—had blamed me for her death. The lashing out, calling people names, running away from home, and talking back during my early teenage years had all contributed to her stress, Nikki said, which eventually led to her death. I believed her. My mind told me that I was a murderer, and that if I had just been a better child, then maybe Aunt Barbara wouldn't have died. Her blood was on my hands, and I couldn't wipe them clean no matter how much I asked God for forgiveness.

With nothing else left to cling on to, my mind replayed the words she had spoken to me that day after my basketball match, again and again.

You mustn't stop following your dreams and being what you want to be. It will all be okay.

I hadn't replied to her that Tuesday night, but I knew now was my chance, even if her body and spirit were no longer physically present in front of me.

"Aunt Barbara, I promise I will make you proud," I whispered. "I promise."

This promise was the only thing I had left. I didn't know what that meant, or what it would look like; I only knew that this promise was one I had to keep.

MARYLAND AND PENNSYLVANIA

The breath of my ancestors lingered here. Under my dusty boots were the blood and tears of enslaved Africans who tried to gain their freedom. In this soil, their blood seeped deeply, ingrained in every particle. We had been brought here, bagged up, and sold. Stomped on, mowed over, and spat on. But in that soil we had planted seeds that grew into mighty trees that withstood time. Those roots now spanned the entire length of the trail, especially in these woods where many had endured and died. This forest was a highway once, a place of rebellion, a place where bodies hung. I felt their energy flowing all around me from the Potomac River into Harpers Ferry, West Virginia.

Harpers Ferry is the headquarters of the Appalachian Trail Conservancy, a famed spot where hikers take pictures and register themselves. I searched through the register. Turtle and the kids were four days ahead; I wondered if I could still catch them. I signed the register and took my picture, sticking my hip out as far to the right as it could go, my rainbow tutu dazzling in the amber glow. It was June, LGBTQIA Pride Month, and I was proud to be out. The tags that year were purple, and I was handed one by one of the volunteers. He wrote the number 420 in a small white rectangle on the back. What a coincidence—a perfect number for a pothead rocking a rainbow tutu.

The trail wound through the historic Old Town section of Harpers Ferry, white blazes carved into the light posts, and passed through John Brown's Fort, the site where John Brown and his followers barricaded themselves in 1859, prepping for an ill-fated rebellion to destroy the institution of slavery. On October 18, 1859, a militia led by Confederate Colonel Robert E. Lee raided the fort, killing ten of Brown's men, capturing six, and trying and hanging them while five others escaped. I went into the fort, picturing the fierce warriors at battle, staring down the face of the enemy, dying to be free.

After the fort, I crossed another bridge that carried me into Maryland. At a scenic overlook in Maryland, ten miles south of the Pennsylvania state line, as I filmed a vlog to post online, I was interrupted by a voice.

"Dragonsky, is that you? Wow! Shit!"

Being approached with such familiarity was now becoming commonplace. On the trail registers I only left a simple *Dragonsky was here* with no date attached, so those who ran into me were startled. My safety was critical. There was word going up the trail that the Proud Boys leader "Enrique" Tarrio had started hiking the trail along with a strange dude named "Rebel" who was known for handing out rebel flags and was threatening to do harm to Black hikers and Black organizations. Needless to say, I had chosen a hell of a year to thru-hike. Being Black marked me as bounty, and I didn't have time to fuck around and find out.

Luckily, this time I had been recognized by a fan and fellow thru-hiker. Their name was Gangsigns. On their backpack, a midsized Puerto Rican flag hung next to a rainbow one, their tails flying freely.

"The reason I follow you on Instagram is because you're the only one out on the trail," Gangsigns said. "Everyone is in the closet, and I respect that you don't hide that you're gay. I'm asexual myself. I didn't expect to see you here, I thought you were way ahead of me."

"Hey! Wait, are you for real? I'm the only one who's out?"

"Yeah, for real! Everyone is, like, scared or something. I'm also from Jersey, by the way. I'm trying to get to Katahdin by the Fourth of July. . . ." They looked at me with eager eyes. "Do you mind if I hike with you?"

I couldn't say no. We fell into a rhythm as we conversed about where we were going and what we had seen. They had been on the trail since April, having started at Springer Mountain in the bubble, the time when the majority of thru-hikers start their hikes, congesting the trail. They were the first person I'd met who was Puerto Rican and asexual. As we hiked, I felt both elated to be in good company and flattered that I had inspired them deeply. They told me that the reason they were hoping to reach Katahdin by the Fourth of July was because their family was throwing a big pig roast that day, and they intended to be there.

"You are totally invited," they told me. "If you can match my pace, that is." I was doubtful. It had become clear pretty quickly that I was the tortoise, and they, the hare.

Maryland was considered a small feat compared to all the other states. But it soon presented itself as a challenge when we attempted to hike through the entire state in twenty-four hours, to our huge regret. Ignorant about Maryland's terrain, we spent the night trying to traverse one of many boulder fields, rolling our ankles constantly.

The AT coincides with the Civil War Trail in Maryland, at one point passing by the graves of a Confederate and Union general, facing each other. The energy of the restless souls in the air was palpable, stronger than the force of gravity. Curious, Gangsigns and I approached the graves to read what was written on the tombstones. As we passed by, a white man who was tending to the grave of the Confederate gave us a disturbed look.

"Can I help you ladies?"

"We're Appalachian Trail thru-hikers, and the trail passes through here. We're just looking at the graves."

"My great-grandfather was buried here. He fought in the Civil War." He was nearly on top of the grave, barring us from viewing it. We got the hint.

"Where are you ladies from?" he asked.

"New Jersey," I said.

"Oh, you mean 'New Joisey'?"

I exchanged a look with Gangsigns. Wrong choice. Nothing makes a New Jerseyan more annoyed than the accent from *The Sopranos*.

"I have never heard anyone who has lived in New Jersey say it that way, have you, Gangsigns?" I said.

"No one says that!" they responded aggressively. "We are a very diverse state—Haitian, Japanese, Jewish, Peruvian, Italian. We all talk differently."

The man put both his hands up in front of him and out to the side, as if he were doing spirit fingers. "Whoa, whoa! I won't do that again. I didn't know. I am sorry to upset you. Have a good day." He backed off, returning to his business.

We continued on. We'd made it halfway through the Appalachian Trail, or at least close. The official midpoint lay ahead at Pine Grove Furnace in Cumberland County, Pennsylvania, notoriously named Rocksylvania. The second-longest state on the AT, PA would be 229 miles of bruised feet, rolled ankles, and sore necks. Boulder fields, jagged rocks, rock ridges, and scrambles gave birth to new challenges, all familiar to me. Pennsylvania had been my training ground before actually getting on the AT—and it was also the last state between me and my home of New Jersey.

When Gangsigns and I were nearing the state line, I received a text. It was Turtle, with some solemn news. They had never planned to make it all the way to Katahdin, and they were planning to get off the trail at the Pennsylvania–New Jersey border for good.

I was too late. I had let them down. They had made space for me and tried to wait for me many times, but I was too far behind. I clutched the phone as if it were my heart. Losing them felt like I was losing part of myself. I felt truly alone even with Gangsigns at my side; I knew that we would eventually separate, too. Soon I would be hiking solo again, to face whatever new challenges arose on the AT by myself.

Ultimately, Turtle and I had both agreed that the Appalachian Trail would not be the end of our tramily—that we would always be tramily, no matter what. My heart knew that we would never truly say goodbye, only *See you later*. As tragic as our unceremonious ending was on the AT, not having the ability to give each other warm hugs and kind words in person, I took a new meaning and lesson from our encounter: to cherish what I had been given, and to carry that love with me to Katahdin. It was time to stand on my own again and continue the journey of finding myself.

Before they got off the trail, Turtle issued me a stern warning. "Be careful of Pen Mar Park. The girls and I went through a lot there. The way they treated my kids was horrible. There's a lot of racism. You should try to see if you can have someone hike through that section with you."

Pen Mar Park were three words I had already heard from the Black thru-hikers I'd spoken to online months before leaving for the AT. I knew it would be a risky section. I relayed my fears to Gangsigns, who agreed to walk with me though Pen Mar. They, too, had experienced racism in their life. It was disheartening to have to depend on another human for my own well-being. I was forced yet again to do the thing I despised, but I swallowed my pride.

At four thirty, we emerged from our green tunnel, crossed over train tracks, and vanished into the forest once again, descending into the cozy darkness. I looked up in awe at the green canopies, dense in their arrangement, determined to block out the sun.

It had taken me all my life to get here. A place where Harriet Tubman had operated the Underground Railroad, guiding the hopeless toward hope. A highway of the oppressed fleeing from the oppressor in the South, their bodies fatigued from the chains that restricted their bodies. Souls could not be chained, and theirs had passed by here. Slavery had sought to beat and break them, their spines enduring lash after lash like the fragile binding of a book. Their cover made them a target, the title on display for all to see. But inside their pages was a story that the oppressor did not want to read. It was their stories that made this sign so significant, not the distracting white font marking the Maryland–Pennsylvania state line at the bottom. I did not care that I was now in Pennsylvania; I only cared about the words MASON–DIXON LINE in the top rectangle.

Gangsigns and I took pictures with the sign and wrote in the register inside the black mailbox that was enclosed in a chimney of neatly stacked rocks. The trail volunteers really knew how to use art in nature. We moved on, making it to Pen Mar Park by the late evening. We came across a clearing that looked out on a blue valley of flatness, where a grotesque, outdated mile marker the size of a movie screen took up the front and center view. The bright sun was losing her glow, and I could barely make out the cars shimmering in the distance below.

We stopped for a couple of hours to rest by the tan building, where there was shade from the awning and the ground was cool. We scarfed down our snacks like hyenas, using the luxury of the

trash can nearby to dispose of our scraps. I had scoped out an outlet
near the bathroom and it took me three hours to charge my battery
pack, though Gangsigns was already raring to go after two. I could
feel them crawling out of their skin like a cicada during the molt. I
wanted to cling on to them, keep them near me; I was afraid to flap
my wings by myself once more. But I had to. After hugging them,
I watched them return home to the woods without me. It was the
last time I saw them.

When my time came, I rose before darkness fell. A quarter mile
up the trail was Falls Creek Campground, and I decided that would
be my stopping point for the night. I scoured the land like a wild
animal, finding the perfect patch to use as my territory. I set up
my tent beneath two big trees whose names I did not care to know,
leaving just enough space for me to crawl through the back door of
the tent. Sitting inside, I groggily inflated my sleeping pad, threw
on my quilt, and curled up on my side. All night I tossed and turned
as the constellations shifted above me.

Branches, lit by the moon, cast shadows, displayed on my tent
as if it were a projector. I could still taste Zuri's lips, feel her arms
around me, and with each passing day I was getting closer to seeing
her again for the first time in five months since I had started on
the AT. She would be picking me up from the trail in Duncannon,
Pennsylvania, and bringing me to Harrisburg for a few days in July.

Duncannon was a place where watching trains go by was a favorite
activity of the locals. There were reports that a thru-hiker had died
shooting up heroin in a hotel, and it wasn't the first overdose that
had occurred there. One hostel, called Kind of Outdoorsy, existed

for hikers, and I sauntered in but ended up turning my back as soon as I saw the "Blue Lives Matter" attire.

When Zuri pulled up, nothing mattered anymore. Jumping up from the bench like a child, I ran to her, throwing myself into the arms of love. We headed back to her hotel in Harrisburg, checked in, and caught up where we'd left off. We got intimate, but something felt off. I could always sense whenever Zuri's heart was not with mine. Our souls spoke a language that needed no translator. Never had I had any such sense with my past partners, leading me to believe that Zuri and I were soulmates. But the sunflowers I had seen in her eyes before seemed to have toppled over, their seeds spilled upon the ground. Losing her petals, only her dark round face remained, the glow gone.

On the second night, in Philly for karaoke at a club, she said to me, "The girl, the one I am messing with, is here. Do you want to meet her?"

My world stopped. I stared at her. Since early June, we'd been having arguments and discussions about this new girl. Zuri didn't even seem to be offering me a choice; no sooner than the words had left her lips did I sense the presence of a stranger five feet away from me, leaning on the stairs. Zuri had a thing for petite African women with stocky bodies, the opposite of her own stature. The darker, the better. Never white girls because "they didn't get us," she said. Zuri's demeanor shifted, our clasped hands now lingering in space. Her eyes became wide as she perked up, her tone softer when she called the other girl's name. The girl came over, arms wide, introducing herself as if we were friends.

I realized I was no longer loved in the way I used to be. I tried to maintain my composure in a room full of strobing blue lights. Heartbreak was watching Zuri interact with this other girl, her invisible hand pushing me away against the wall. Once I had been her priority; now I was only an option. And yet, the idea of giving up on us seemed impossible to me. With nowhere to run, I reached for Zuri's hand, merely surviving.

"You're spending a lot of time with her," I said.

"It's just fun. We're just having fun," she said, something she repeated every time.

Going around in circles was getting tiresome. I'd been faithful to her all along, pleading with her to end this.

"Just take me back to the trail," I said.

"Fine. Will I see you at my birthday in two weeks?"

"Sure . . . I guess . . . if I'm in New Jersey by then. I can take the train to Philly."

After a brief kiss, she started up the car, and we left the club. The next day, Zuri drove me back to the trail.

Staring out the window, I saw a reflection of myself—a glass figurine, fragile shards glued together like a high school project. She let me out. It was time to go home to the mountains.

It was hell. First days back on trail after a few zeros always were. My heart weighed more than my pack. Trudging up each hill, laboring hard, bug-eyed and hopeless, I marched on. Beneath the canopies were curtains of trunks, the rising and falling of the mountains, a sea of rocks. I wanted to pry them out, throw them at the trees, and show them how mad I was. I wanted to unveil the grasses that the rocks had strangled. I needed some green in this goddamn forest! These rocks were useless; most I had to straddle, throwing one leg over the other, pulling my pack straps tight. Rocking the boat too hard could turn me upside down like a turtle. I screamed and wailed from the tops of the mountains, their bony ridges catching my faltering spirit. A boundless vista marked with white blazes, once a world of wonder and awe, became a private world of weariness and woe.

For two weeks, I sang "Lonesome Dreams" by Lord Huron. He understood my aching heart. Lord Huron was by my side during the great rock assault of Pennsylvania, and together we climbed in and out of Port Clinton, scaling the near-vertical scramble at Palmerton, the white blazes only appearing when the back of my head touched my back as I glanced up. Rattlesnakes and rocks, a constant battle of *kill or be killed*, that's all Pennsylvania was. Lots of hikers crawled on their hands and knees into New Jersey, their feet bruised. There were no pleasant rewards, no scenic or memorable vistas, no national parks or forests in Pennsylvania—just hell, and barely any potable water. The towns were lacking; it seemed the locals weren't too amenable to hikers or Black people. While trying to leave Michaux State Forest around six p.m., a local at the shelter told me, "Honey, you can't leave. This is a sundown town. The cops will kill you and cover it up."

In 2021.

But in the rocky outcropping there was always a silver lining. I met two phenomenal people by random chance in the great rock garden. One was a former thru-hiker named Woodnymph, who had long wild hair and wore hippie skirts and tie-dye shirts. I met her right after Palmerton, the trail deciding to intervene and send me a friend, and we did some straight-up weird shit. While I was alone with Lord Huron on Palmerton, the clouds decided to spill their buckets upon my head. Rock and water were not my favorite combination, by any means. They always said you were not a real thru-hiker unless you "shit your pants," and I was nearly shitting as the thunder started coming in, but the adrenaline kept me going. When I descended and told Woodnymph what I'd achieved, she said, "I did Palmerton southbound in a rainstorm." I guess my small feat wasn't shit. Woodnymph was tough, hiked with her kitten on her shoulder, and showed me a secret waterfall near Jim Thorpe where we camped for the night. She had started to set up her tent when all of a sudden I was disturbed by a deep wailing. I was not sure whether it was her cat or her.

"WHERE'S MY FUCKING FLASHLIGHT? OH MY FUCKING GOD!"

Her head collapsed in her hands as her mouth went off. "OH MY GOD! GOD, I JUST HAD IT! I CAN'T FUCKING BELIEVE THIS— JASPER, STOP! WHAT DO I DO NOW? FUCK!" With full lungs, she released her SOS call into the abyss, where not even the roaring of the water could subdue it. My immediate thoughts were that this white girl was wild, and what the fuck did I get myself into? I decided to back away slowly from the wails of what sounded like the Jersey Devil reincarnated and give her space. But after a quick chat with her girlfriend on the phone, she fell calm, drank some whiskey, and danced the night away to Celtic music. I wasn't sure if I wanted to rip my eardrums out or bang my head against a rock; it was that terrible. Yet our friendship continued to grow, and I came to accept this wild woman with the lungs of a whale. She was weird and had a mental illness like me; she was family.

Then there was Coyote, a young white man who picked me up on a hitch that I was reluctant to take. At first glance, his shiny bald white head told me to back the fuck off. When I got near the car, he introduced himself.

"Hey thru-hiker! You need a ride?" he said with a warm smile. "I know what you're thinking, it's that look on your face. You think I'm a skinhead. Please, it's not that."

"Then what is it, sir? I have had some bad hitches," I said. I learned from my mistakes.

"I have prostate cancer and lost all my hair," he said, his voice fading out a little. I was hit with sympathy for him, and my instinct told me that he seemed okay. I got in the car, and he offered to take me to his tiny apartment to make me lunch. I was hesitant to follow another white man to his house and possibly risk my life, but there was a draw to him. I followed my soul. He was kind and young, in his thirties, his warm eyes making me lower my shield. We talked the night away, and he offered to slackpack me through Michaux State Forest. He was elated to see me doing what I was doing as a Black woman and even offered to donate two thousand dollars to support my thru-hike. Money was something I never liked to take from white folks out of fear that they would eventually turn on me and say I owed them something, whether it be a bargain for subservience or to stay silent and not talk about my Blackness. Coyote proved to be different; he was genuine.

"Cancer was the best thing that happened to me. It taught me how to enjoy and live life to the fullest. I am much more grateful. Please, I want to help support your journey. I am in remission now and nearly cancer-free, I have so much to give." And so I accepted his cash and his friendship.

Pennsylvania, separated from my home state by only the Delaware River, was the Tennessee of the North. Quite a depressing place, really. And nothing was more depressing than taking on the obstacles alone. It was not how it should have been. Never had I envisioned crossing my state line without Turtle, Bobo, Jumprope, and Grumpy Cat. It should have been a homecoming, a celebration, a way to share my world with them. Instead of hugs and goodbyes, all I had were texts on my cell phone. *Could have, should have, would have.*

No one walked beside me. No one to take me home. I was a flower, buried under the first season's snow, awaiting the sun to release me. But my head could not stay buried for too long. Holding my face up to the clouds, I rose from the ground, feeling the warmth of summer. Bees came like sunny daydreams, blessing each flower, balls of golden pollen clinging to their hind legs. They carried a piece of each flower with them into the wide blue sky, aware that the seasons would change. That winter would come again and again, that flowers would once again lie dormant, but that inside the hive, the heart of the bees would beat harder than ever.

The queen could not die. She had work to do.

FIRST QUARTER MOON

After my aunt's passing, I vowed to live a life that would reflect everything she had taught me. But life would never be the same. Family stopped getting together, and my uncle remarried and sold the ranch-style house with the purple shutters that I had been so fond of. Saying goodbye was heartbreaking, and I had to grow up faster than I should have. But I knew that I had to keep going for my aunt. She was watching over me, and I knew no matter what came my way, I had to fight—because she would have wanted me to.

Fight through the lonely days when I would come home and there would be a void. Fight through the loneliness when my cousin and her boyfriend started living with my uncle, while he went back and forth to North Carolina. Fight through milestones that tore me apart, when I knew my aunt would not attend my high school graduation and eventually my graduation with a bachelor's degree in social work from Rutgers, where I made dean's list three times. How hard it was to walk through the stadium seeing the faces of my mother, uncle, sister, and a plethora of family and friends but knowing there was a face missing. She never got to see me get my driver's license and first car. I never got to tell her that I studied abroad in China for a summer and helped the Roma children at the orphanage in Cluj-Napoca, Romania.

Holidays became insignificant and impacted my mental health severely. Thanksgiving was hard, but I decided to spend it with my friends and my mother occasionally. Christmas, however, for the first time in my life, sent me down a rabbit hole of depression. The sound of Christmas music triggered flashbacks of when I had spent Christmas with my aunt. Toasted chestnuts in a flowered glass-plated bowl that sat in the dining room under the chandelier I had once cut my head on. Red, white, and green decorative icicles that adorned the house, and within it my family eating breakfast and opening gifts. Those days were long gone, and I sank into a dark depression every holiday season. I hibernated like a bear with no desire to catch fish, climb trees, or really survive. The safety of the den was where I stayed until spring came, jolting the earth back to life, awakening the animals from their winter slumber to celebrate the birth of a new cycle.

As a kid, losing my aunt meant losing my whole world, my structure, support, and guidance. But eventually a germinated seed will push through the tough soil, and I could not stay buried under the dirt. So I took matters into my own hands as I grew into an adult. I learned how to cook, write checks, go grocery shopping, and drive a car. Becoming self-sufficient was something I started to strive for.

It was 2014 when I graduated from Rutgers University. I had settled on a bachelor's degree in social work under the illusion that I liked helping people. In fact, I hated people, but I could not do the math to grant me passage into the field that I truly desired to join: veterinary medicine. Fresh out of college, I worked in a field that I could not bear for a few years. My clients' stories of trauma and resilience both captivated me and burned me out. Job after job slipped through my fingers. Anxiety and depression caused me to be late for work often, made me think that everyone was my enemy, and told me that I would inevitably fuck everything up and that no one would like me. Concealing my mental disabilities from my employer became commonplace, as I didn't want to risk not being hired at all, but time and time again, eventually the veil fell off.

After I was fired from one social work job for having a panic attack at work, I decided to look into AmeriCorps. On a whim I decided it would be a stellar idea to pack up all my things and move halfway across the country to Austin, Texas, to join AmeriCorps to become a science teacher. Out of a few other locations I could select from, including a Peace Corps posting in Ukraine and the Japan Exchange and Teaching Program in Japan, I chose fire ants and an outdoor oven that fried eggs on the sidewalk during the summer months. Little did I know how AmeriCorps operated. We were supposed to do over one thousand hours of service throughout our term, including mandatory weekend service, whether that be setting up a career fair or helping dig out garden beds. Office work was scheduled in the mornings and teaching was meant for the afternoon. I had been working since I was fifteen years old, and the stipend they gave us was insufficient for living expenses. A lot of us had issues affording groceries and making time for ourselves, and balancing it all was straining.

Lesson planning proved to be more challenging than I thought, and we had tight deadlines. We were assigned different courses to teach, and I landed Animal Behavior, Chemistry, Youth Gardening, and Robotics, the last of which I hated with a fiery passion. Before we could officially teach, we had to demonstrate a run-through of our lesson in front of our peers. I nearly lost my lunch that day. I was too shy and scared to talk to anyone. Making friends was hard for me in general, but making friends in a new state was harder.

Additionally, the depressive thoughts refused to cease. It wasn't getting better, only worse. My history of sexual abuse and family abandonment led to severe body dysmorphic disorder. Getting carried away was all too common once stuck in the sea of toxic thoughts, and every inch of my body was a canvas; every cut told a story. My arms took a brutal assault, each cut marking the pain of sexual trauma, and I soon moved to my breasts, as these were breasts that men had sexualized before I even knew what they were. The cuts were shallow, just like those men were. Meanwhile, my thighs took on the eternal pain of neglect. Neglect burned deep within me. To not be wanted, and told that I was not wanted throughout my childhood, was especially difficult. Deep gashes in the top of my thigh spelled out the word *DEATH*. There was something appealing in those deep, scarlet, bloody letters that I had spent twenty minutes meticulously trying to imprint in the fat of my thighs. I was satisfied because I could see my pain, touch it, smell its pungency.

Staying in treatment had never been an issue for me, but my mental disorders reared their heads regardless. It did not matter if I complied with my medication, therapy, nutrition, or exercise schedule; there was no mercy. My brain felt like a building, collapsing upon itself tenfold, leaving no room for escape. Buried under the rubble, covered in ash and debris, I was unrecognizable. Depression was an abscess swelling up with more pus and fluid day by day, leaving me with the option of enduring the pain until the skin ruptured or taking matters into my own hands and lancing it with a scalpel.

Many times, I tried to ask for help from friends and the queer-friendly church community I was a part of in Austin, only to get ignorance thrown into my face. Jayson, a tall, dark, gay, and flamboyant Black man, was someone I considered a friend from church. But when I reached out to him to tell him I was depressed, he dismissed my feelings.

"It's all a mindset. If you think positive, then you will manifest positivity in your life. But you . . . you sit here, and you want people to feel sorry for you. Well, I don't. You need to stay positive, and clearly you aren't."

He had seen my multiple Facebook posts about my depression. His statement was one that I was accustomed to. He was a Black man, and he was raised the same way I was. If he struggled outwardly, he would potentially be berated by his homeboys. He would feel emasculated if he was viewed as weak or vulnerable, because, after all, the Black man was supposed to be as strong as an ox: He endured the lashings of the whip on his back. He worked long and hard in the fields picking cotton. He provided for his family and triumphed over the white man.

In the absence of communal support, I sought out the professionals.

"I really do not think that this drug is working for me . . . and I think about dying a lot. I am scared," I told the doctor. I had no emotions, no feelings, no desire for pleasure or food. I had just told my psychiatrist—my sixth—that Viibryd was making me have thoughts of ending my life. At the time Viibryd was new, and it would be my twenty-fifth drug to trial to see if it was able to control my increasing depressive symptoms. I was not fond of newer drugs because the full side effects were not all known.

I had become a walking pharmacy and advocate for myself. Abilify and Lamictal did nothing. Lithium only made me paranoid and see things that were not there. Dark shadowy apparitions appeared in my doorway, on the windowsill, and even hunching over my body. Lexapro and Zoloft made me feel like a slimy, slow, dull slug. Cymbalta and Effexor made me straight-up want to die, and now Viibryd destroyed my very being, turning me against myself. I felt like a human test dummy waiting to be used again and again without producing any results.

"Just give it a few more days to work," my psychiatrist reassured me. I didn't want to give it a few more days, though; Viibryd already had me on a self-destructive path.

Three days later, on a clear Thursday night, I found myself in the parking lot of CVS. There were a few other cars parked; however, they were no concern of mine. Worthlessness, failure, and feelings of self-hatred manifested stronger than they ever had in the past.

You're so stupid, Shilletha. No one likes you, can't you see that? All your friends and family don't even talk to you. It's all because you're a burden. You can't do anything right.

This time, I was ready and prepared to end my life with no thoughts of regret. The fear of death was long gone. The grave became my obsession. I longed for my own end.

I sauntered into the pharmacy. A still sensation pulsed from the roots of my unkempt ear-length dreads to the soles of my feet. I picked up my pace as if I were driven by an engine and found what I was looking for—razors. I grabbed a pack of three and headed to the register. Razors in hand, I began to glide as one does on skates—freedom was near, and the stakes were too high. Turning back would be pointless now. Back in my car, I began to dismantle the razor, digging out the blades using my silver pocketknife. Piece by piece, the white plastic collected like sand against the grain of my carpeted floor mats.

Devoid of hope, I sank into my sorrow and surrendered. My cuts were shallow and superficial rather than wide and deep. I didn't want to die, I just wanted to feel. Numbness is a dangerous feeling; it drives the empty soul into utter chaos. When you're so void, you want to feel anything—though *anything* isn't ever enough.

I finished up with my self-harming episode. A blanket of relief came over me. Half a mile was the distance I had to drive from the pharmacy to the dam. I headed for the bridge that rose over the dam. People in cars drove by with no inkling of what I was about to do, and why would they? By the time some of us are ready to end our lives, we give off no signals, as we wish for no interference. We have settled our grievances, written our goodbye letters, and even given away our most prized possessions and materials. At the end of the day, those materials and items we own bear no merit in the grave. Death does not discriminate; it is not greedy; it is not concerned with the luxuries of life. As with a hurricane, there is usually a calm before the storm.

Godspeed, Shilletha.

Approaching the bridge gave me chills. The dam at night reminded me to fear. The dark water gave no hints to its depths or the creatures that lay within. Bodies of water at night terrified me: No one can see you, few can hear you, and if something happened, who would go into the mysterious giant sinkhole to save you? At the same time, my logic was that I did not want to be found.

The only barrier between the dam and me was a rusty wire fence. I was on the seesaw between life and death. I had been robbed of so many years of pleasure, socialization, sleep, nourishment, and, quite frankly, function. Depression left untreated or on the wrong concoction of medications can and will result in a loss of life. At that very moment, depression had me hanging off the ledge, asking my brain, *Why are you doing this to me?*

As I contemplated my question, my phone rang. One call went by and I ignored it, but there was only so much ignoring I could do. It rang six more times. It was Pepper, my girlfriend at the time, so I finally answered.

"Babe, where the fuck are you? Shilletha . . . WHERE THE FUCK ARE YOU!?" she screamed loudly. Horrified, she continued to press me for answers. "I am so worried about you—where are you? You better tell me now! Right now!"

"I walked to the bridge because—"

"SHILLETHA, YOU BETTER GET YOUR ASS HERE RIGHT NOW! I need you, please don't do this. What is going on? What the hell . . ."

Hesitantly, I told her about my medication change and the suicidal thoughts. I told her about being overwhelmed with work and life and feeling like nothing. We must have gone back and forth for about ten minutes before she persuaded me to come home with offers of sex and food. She always knew how to get me back: If I didn't want sex . . . well, then all hope would be lost. I needed her touch to feel alive at a time when I was walking in death.

Backing off that cold metal rung was painful. My past ten or so suicide attempts had been agony beyond the worst physical illness you can imagine: to have to come home and realize that the next day when you wake up to the realities of the world, your brain is going to start the morning with a direct threat to your life. Thoughts of being a burden, of being unloved and without value, would again start their relentless attacks. Then there was the thought of returning to AmeriCorps the next day where I was working, carrying the frozen weight of Mount Everest and having to put on a happy face so I could interact with others in an appropriate manner. Pepper held me throughout the night and silenced the mess that was in my head, but I knew a storm was brewing, and there was no shelter to burrow in.

13

NEW JERSEY AND NEW YORK

Walls of green embosomed me, lavishing me with gold emblems from the sun. Towering over the river, Mount Tammany took center stage. There was nothing on the Appalachian Trail that mimicked her; she had no parallel, with her ribbons of quartzite. She rose from New Jersey, while her elegant sister, Mount Minsi, dominated Pennsylvania. Divided by the Delaware River and Interstate 80, they formed the Delaware Water Gap. Home was in the valley on that interstate where normal people drove to normal places with wheels instead of walking across the country. They traveled in their unnatural objects, parking on the side to climb Mount Tammany in flip-flops and sandals.

A radiating pain in my left ankle had kept me up the previous night, popping like the cork of a wine bottle. I was concerned. Other hikers dealt with their pain with "vitamin I," ibuprofen, and so I popped two—my first on trail. Eventually, they said, my ankle pain would go away. I also knew that rest would be coming soon—my friend Dani was waiting to pick me up in the parking lot of the Delaware Water Gap National Recreation Area. But more important than any of that, I was coming to a milestone in my journey.

The rocky trail descended Mount Minsi steeply into the gap. A wide riverbed flowed below, twisting through the valley in an S shape. In the air, the sweet aroma of new life bloomed in the leafy forest. The small town of Delaware Water Gap is known for its hospitality for hikers, but I bypassed it, eager to get to my state line. The sight of the cream road barriers excited me, and, almost forgetting my ankle, I wanted to run at it at full speed with my pack on my back.

The state line was painted like a flag divided into three strips— yellow, white, green. It could only be accessed by foot. The green strip represented Pennsylvania; the yellow, New Jersey. Katahdin became tangible, within arm's reach, 895 miles. No longer was I the same person who had crossed the state line on my first backpacking trip, months ago now. Nature had made me the person I'd become and the person I aspired to be. Each step I took was sure, wild rivers in my eyes, the sun smiling back with its eternal light. With a purple sports bra, black shorts, and the ultimate tan, I pulled my GoPro out of my front pocket and began recording my milestone, choking back tears, cars honking from the highway.

"WHOOOOOOOO! I made it home! What a big freaking

accomplishment!" I yelled, waving my trekking poles at my side, clipping my face. "YES! Yes, yes. Yes, oh my god! PA, we're done. This is a fucking amazing day."

I continued over a bridge, questioning its structural soundness as it trembled beneath my feet, the heat from the concrete rising through the soles of my shoes. The sun was high, shimmering like boiling water, her rays melting my skin into puddles of chocolate. Just over the bridge was the wonderful world of diners and good pizza, Wawa, hoagies, diversity, and acceptance. And best of all, Black people.

Godspeed, Dragonsky. Godspeed.

Drivers passing through my state on Interstate 95 via the NJ Turnpike were jaded and ill-informed. New Jersey has always been the brunt of everyone's jokes, commonly referred to as "dirty" and "loaded with cities." My favorite response whenever I tell people who aren't from New Jersey that I am indeed from New Jersey is "Oh . . . I'm sorry." Sorry for what? We aren't Alabama, Florida, or, even worse, Texas—we're way better than that. We're blunt as fuck, and we don't take anyone's bullshit. That's the beauty of my state: There's a realness to it, authenticity in the hearts of the people.

And no, we don't pump our own gas.

I knew New Jersey in the most intimate way. I knew New Jersey more than most New Jerseyans knew New Jersey. I knew Wawa, pork roll, and eggs and cheese on an everything bagel at 7:55 a.m., right before settling in to work. I've roller-skated at Branch Brook Park and ate at the James Beard–nominated pizza shop Razza in Jersey City. I've skimboarded at Long Beach Island along the sandy beach and counted blackjack cards in Atlantic City. But that wasn't all. There were hidden treasures in the pine forests of the south and the silver of the Appalachian Mountains in the north. I knew the plump blackberries, highbush blueberries, mulberries, and wineberries. I knew the black gum tree and how its branches stuck out parallel to the ground. Oh, how I adored the soft leaves of the mullein plant; a professor of mine once even said, "That's what I want my underwear made of."

Musical trills radiated through those forests, the star singer the goldfinch, our state bird. The downy woodpecker joined in with hard knocks on the wood, as if to ask whether anyone was home. Deer grazed and galloped at the sound of a pin drop. Thousands of docile black bears roamed the Kittatinny Mountains, unburdening the forest of her heavenly, succulent berries. Then there were the green ferns, the feathers of the forest, a prehistoric emblem of all of time existing before our very eyes. Chanterelles, chicken of the woods, purple mushrooms, and ones that looked like Toad from *Super Mario* thrived in this forager's paradise. Worthington, Stokes, Wawayanda, and High Point state forests, seventy-two miles of brilliant views, open ridge walks, serene lakes, glacier ponds, singing bullfrogs, and the most road crossings I'd ever cross. Stairway to Heaven, the Boardwalk, Sunfish Pond, Raccoon Ridge—New Jersey had the best names, in my biased opinion, of notable landmarks.

And so I walked into the Garden State, more prideful than I had ever been. I contacted my friend Dani, who wanted to greet me as soon as I crossed the state line. When I arrived at the parking lot,

Dani nearly pushed me to the ground with a snug hug. She offered to take me to Tops Diner in East Newark, my absolute favorite and one of the top diners in the nation. My mind went into the clouds, picturing what I would consume within the next hour. Not burgers—I found them repulsive, and red meat made my colon hurt. *Pasta*, I thought, *I want to eat pasta.*

Dani was glowing, her hair falling down to her shoulders, a smile as wide as a rainbow on her face. "So tell me about the trail, dude!" she insisted. *Bro* was usually the term preferred in New Jersey, but I loved the way she said *dude*. Dani put her hands under her chin and looked up at me.

"First of all, you're a badass!"

I began to speak, but she cut me off.

"Second of all, how has your hike been? You should be proud!"

"Well, I started by—"

"AND WHAT'S YOUR FAVORITE PLACE SO FAR?"

I laughed and just let Dani get all her questions out. I drank a bottled water and checked my messages while she talked and talked . . . and talked some more. I ordered a massive plate of fettuccine alfredo and a cookies-and-cream milkshake. Dani ordered a two-egg platter, toast, three strips of bacon, and crispy breakfast potatoes. My pasta was perfectly al dente, the heavy cream and parmesan getting bolder with every bite. The milkshake was divine. The combination of dairy would later disrupt the bowels, but for now, I had to indulge.

After lunch, Dani and I went back to her place to get ready for her friend's birthday that night. I was invited.

"But I don't have anything to wear. All I have are my hiker clothes," I protested.

"It's fine, dude. No one is going to care. You're badass, you're hiking across the country."

Dani spent two hours in the bathroom dressing herself up like a china doll. Back and forth she ran to the closet. "How does this look?" she asked. I told her she looked beautiful, but that did not settle with her. She kept putting on clothes and taking them off. Finally the chaos ended, and we took a hit of a much-needed blunt.

We drove to the party. Once we arrived, I suddenly felt out of place. Music boomed through the speakers. Humans mingled with each other, dressed casually but with good taste. I wanted nothing to do with their luxuries, this luxury. Nothing felt right. Trying to socialize felt harder than climbing a mountain. I wanted to go home.

"I haven't gotten out much," I explained to one partygoer.

"That's COVID for ya. It's been so difficult."

It wasn't about COVID. It was about something that no one else understood. A new place they could not comprehend, a garden of mountains and leafy forests, cooing winds, and rushing rivers. Life was no longer about the eighty-dollar Tommy Hilfiger shirt or the five-bedroom house with a maid. I wanted items that could not be bought, at least to some extent. The culture shock frightened me, as if I had never known the life I had had prior to doing the AT. I hung out in awkward places in the room, a dark empty corner, then on the arm of a couch, distracted by the pings from my phone.

It was Zuri. We were texting back and forth, and she agreed to meet me here. It took her thirty minutes to get to the party in an Uber. I took her hand and we went inside, but there was still a distance between us, a raging river.

That night we all went back to Dani's place. Zuri wrapped me up in her arms on a couch meant for one. I lay on top of her, my head resting on her heart, my thoughts racing to the plans we had made for the next few days. Zuri was going to a lesbian summer bash on a boat at the pier in Philadelphia for her twenty-ninth birthday, and I had agreed to take time off from the trail to accompany her. I couldn't stand to miss such an important event, but my heart thudded at the knowledge that I wouldn't be the only one.

A few days later, joined by our mutual friend Alicia, we booked an elegant Airbnb for one night with beds and air-conditioning in the center of the city. Although the beds were soft, I couldn't get comfortable. The air conditioner, in contrast to the wind's natural breeze, felt like an imposter. This wasn't my home. The walls that we stayed in made me antsy. I wanted to break free.

For her party, Zuri wore a violet tutu and sun hat. I went to a thrift store and landed short black shorts that cuffed my butt, making it look supple and juicy, with a black top that zipped up halfway, revealing my cleavage. The boat was filled with gorgeous women with outfits I envied. Comparing myself to them made me feel god-awful. I felt ugly. We danced as soon as we hit the floor, Alicia taking the night.

Suddenly, a knot, a solid ball of dough, formed in my stomach. The silhouette of the other girl, the girl I had been forced to meet a few weeks earlier, appeared as the record played.

I braced for impact. The intimacy, the look in their eyes, created a new song. A strange chorus, a nightmare of sorts. Each touch, the closeness of their lips, spoke multitudes. It consumed me. Zuri had once looked at me like that, before, as if I were the morning and evening star, but now there were brighter stars in the sky.

Friends? I scoffed. *Friends don't do that. Friends don't touch up on each other the way they do. Friends with benefits don't hold hands . . . don't nearly kiss in front of me.*

Zuri never took notice of the sun setting within me, the light dimming. The dance floor became silent amid the chaos, and in that silence, I walked away. For a moment, I felt like I was doing the right thing, but a riveting black hole pulled my curious eyes back. What I saw changed me forever. They were intertwined. Those same gentle hands that had cuddled me to sleep were now exploring another woman's body. There was no shame.

That was when I knew it was over.

Alicia saw me frozen and swept me into her safe embrace. She listened and offered advice. I clung to every word. Lava built up inside me, ready to erupt. I had to stand up to Zuri. I didn't want to lose Zuri, but I refused to lose myself.

Strangers glanced at my face, stained from my charcoal-black mascara. The makeup that had aided my confidence now revealed the true me. I pushed on Zuri, and Zuri pushed back:

"I didn't know you were watching.

"We're just friends having fun.

"You ruined my birthday party!"

Zuri was ready to move on. I was a chewed piece of gum, now stuck under a bench. While I had loved her like no other, her love

152

waxed and waned like the moon, caught between the tides of love and lust. There was always a dark side to the moon, and I saw it that day among the twinkling stars. I would not be part of this cycle, not any longer.

When the party ended, the energy in the car was awkward as hell. We could not stand to be near one another as I sobbed through the darkest night of my journey. I wept, for I knew that this would be the last time we would exist under the same sky, the same sun and moon. This was our goodbye.

Morning came, gray clouds heavy with rain, and I was ready to go back to the trail, finish what I had started, leave everything else behind.

I had already done Worthington State Forest and a few others for practice before I came to the trail, and so I would be redoing a section I had hiked back in December and January. In summer, New Jersey is an earthbound hell. Bloodthirsty vampires come in different forms: the mosquitoes, the big-mouthed blackflies, and the gnats. Choose your poison. I had Alicia drop me off at Dunnfield Creek, where the trail awaited, the clear, crisp water flowing down the banks. I knew this place. It was my favorite state forest in New Jersey, and Zuri and I had had our first hike here in five feet of snow last year.

This time I wouldn't be hiking it alone, either; my friend Liz from New Jersey wanted to join me for a section of trail from Delaware Water Gap to Sunfish Pond. I was grateful. The woods, once my place of refuge, had become a place of sorrow in the aftermath of Zuri, and I needed a friend. And so I found myself waiting in the parking area, watching a green truck pull into the U-shaped lot, dozens of people walking past with children and dogs. Liz was tinier than when I had seen her last; she had always had some meat on her bones.

"Hey, ma! I am so happy to see you. Thank you for letting me join you."

"You got everything you need?" I asked.

"Yeah, I've got a new tent, a new pack, and some food. I am ready to do this!"

I pictured us strolling down the trail, conversing about our lives. This was the easiest part of New Jersey. There were no steep ups and downs, just baby steps. A gradual climb in the deep fern wilderness. But to my surprise, Liz had no idea what she was in for. Her backpack was longer than she was, sagging to the ground. In her right hand she carried a spray bottle that had a daisy-shaped fan attached to its head. "Ma, it's so hot . . . oh my god," she repeated. "How do you do this, oh my god!"

Truly, I didn't know how I did. Heat melted my brain, my ambitions, and my will to continue on as the mosquitoes denied me rest. By now water sources were far behind us at Mt. Minsi and Dunnfield. Our next source would come at a spring by Sunfish Pond, if we ever got there. Liz talked loudly, her voice floating through the trees. At least she had weed.

Every ten feet, we stopped so she could relieve herself from the angry sun. It was slow moving, the slowest I'd gone on trail. Irritation crossed my mind, but I blew it out to the wind; she was new to this. We all had to start somewhere.

It took us three hours to get two miles down the trail to a clearing where an informational board and register box greeted us. Rivulets of sweat poured down Liz's back, her hair clinging to her salty face. The dark gray clouds above were relaying their own alerts, ones that I never ignored. The wind shifted slightly.

"We're going to stop here and wait for the storm to pass, okay? I am going to set my tent up and take a nap."

Liz agreed, and we went down the hill behind the sign to find ample tent spots. Within three minutes, my tent was properly staked and set up, while she was struggling.

"This is a new tent, I have never used it. Ma, I need help!"

There's this saying that in case of an emergency in an airplane, the oxygen masks may drop down, and you should put your mask on first before attending to children or others. With the storm barreling down, I had to be selfish. My gear had to last me the rest of the trail. I was the one who had to wake up the next day and continue down the trail while my friend returned to civilization. Liz looked miserable, and her grunts and moans made me feel bad. Once I got my tent up, I did help Liz with her car camping tent. How much weight was she carrying? We had only gone car camping together; that was her niche. The sky crashed and crackled, illuminated by lighting. While I went into a deep slumber, Liz waited out the storm, chain-smoking cigarettes and pacing. Two hours later when the world was calm again, she wanted to get back on trail, unaware of how my life worked.

"What time is it?" I said groggily.

"Five p.m., ma! Let's go!"

"I need to rest. It's been such a hard weekend. I feel depressed . . . I'll go on tomorrow."

The hardest thing to explain to the people we call day hikers, the ones who go on hikes during the day and who return at night, is sleep. Whenever a storm came in, I set up my tent and slept. If I woke up in the morning during a rainstorm, it was back to the sack. Liz couldn't grasp this notion, and the boredom annoyed her. I went back to sleep, assuming that Liz would, too. Wrong. The sun rose around six thirty a.m. the next day, and Liz was pacing throughout the camp.

"Ma, I can't do this. This is so hard. I didn't sleep at all last night. I want to go home."

I tried to think of a bailout. We could go back the way we came or take a side trail to the left down to the road. Before I could decide, an ATC trail runner volunteer arrived. He was stationed at the informational board to assist thru-hikers with any questions they might have, warning them that fires weren't allowed and giving them tips about bear safety. Little did he know he was about to become a hero. Liz and I chatted with him, and upon hearing about Liz's misery, he offered to hike with her back to her car. I wanted to go with them, too; my mojo was gone. All three of us descended the small mountain and got back to the car within an hour and a half. Liz and I hugged each other, and I departed. I was back on my own.

Nostalgia flooded my world as I thru-hiked across my state. Many of my friends offered help in the form of free rides, food, and their homes along the way. These good deeds are known as trail magic. Around every corner, random people cook and go the distance to help thru-hikers out of the goodness of their hearts. Pizza, Wawa, bagels—you name it, my friends brought it. Sunrise Mountain was the best trail magic I ever had. A Dragonfly who was fighting her battle with cancer drove two hours from Philadelphia to Sunrise Mountain to set up a table of Jersey's finest hoagies and bagels for me. New Jersey spoiled me, and saying goodbye was hard. Being at home while on trail offered up the allure of friends and family begging for my time. But homesickness could not keep me here, I knew; I had to move on before one of my friends shot a tranquilizing dart at me and dragged me into their basement, taking my gear, forcing me to stay.

Farewell, NJ, I thought as I placed my hand on the boulder that had the state line written in chalk. It was here where I felt the true sting of hurt. I was in the rocky abyss, alone with my thoughts and my broken heart. Suddenly, nothing mattered anymore. I forgot all about the trail magic and my friends. I believed no one loved me, and I didn't love myself. Love was my worth, the degree I was seeking. It was also one of my biggest triggers. Letting someone else define my worth with their love, or lack of love, was destroying me. There, I stood in the rain and let it pummel me.

I set up my tent somewhere off the beaten path. Rumination, one of depression's comrades, paid me a visit. My brain was a traffic circle, a car that kept going round and round, unable to get off at an exit. *I am a piece of shit*, that was all I could think about. My mind was lost in time. I forgot who I was. *I'd rather rot in my tent than anything. I hope that no one discovers me. No one will know I'm here. I've chosen a secluded tent site. Out of sight, out of mind.* I popped two anxiety pills and called it a day, ready to go to sleep even though the sun was still high in the sky.

"Hey!" A man's voice echoed through the woods. "I recognize that pack and that tent!"

That voice was one I had heard hundreds of times, one that had leapfrogged me up the trail. I stuck my head out of the tent, forgetting my glasses, but I still knew who it was despite the sea of blur.

"Chai, is that you?"

"You betcha, and Mocha, too!"

I had not expected to see them at all; they had gotten off in New Jersey for an event back home. Little did they know that they were my angels, always showing up whenever I needed someone the most, and for that reason, I loved them. Their presence reminded me that someone cared about my well-being . . . someone cared about my presence here on Earth. Just two familiar faces made a difference in my mood. We spoke briefly, and I was sure that we would see each other again.

The encounter filled me with the energy to pack up my tent and keep moving up the trail. It was only one o'clock, far too early for any hiker to retire for the night.

I came to a waterfall. Taking a break to enjoy its beauty, I sat on a wet rock to collect water to filter. As I took it all in, another hiker joined me. She was short like me and had a pair of binoculars around her neck.

"How are you? I'm Bluebird. What's your name?" she said.

"Hey, I'm Dragonsky, and I—"

"Wait, you're Dragonsky? My sister has been talking about you! She follows you on Instagram. She's a huge fan of yours. She's just ahead of us."

Her eyes gleamed. I was flattered and asked if I could join her. She said yes, and just like that, we were off. We hiked for a mile and ran into Bluebird's sister, Jinx, reclining on her backpack against a small hill on the left side of the trail. Under her cap, sassafras leaves drooped like basset hound ears to the base of her jawline. The combination of her red wavy hair and green sassafras leaves made her look festive. We decided to take a short lunch break before meeting up with their father, Pushcushion, who was two miles ahead. Bluebird ate a tuna wrap, Jinx a few granola bars, and I dove into a tortilla with a Split, a packet of almond butter and jelly weighing under two ounces. I carried many of these instead of the bulky individual jars that I had seen with some hikers.

After lunch, we joined Pushcushion. He was also wearing ears made out of sassafras leaves under his cap. I didn't understand this fashion trend, and my curiosity finally broke through.

"Why do you wear sassafras leaves?" I asked.

"They help repel the mosquitoes. They don't like the chemicals in sassafras. It's worked for me so far. It keeps them out of my ears, too."

I had studied the sassafras tree in community college in my ecology class. The leaves had three distinct shapes—the mitt, the club, and the glove. I couldn't recall it being talked about as a repellent, but wanting to be hip, I added some leaves to my hat and joined in with the fun. Our destination that day was Harriman State Park, where we were planning to set up camp early and get some quality rest.

Once we arrived, we scouted out ideal campsites. A sea of shards shimmered in the setting sun—everywhere was littered with glass. We did our best to avoid puncturing our gear with the litter, let alone our feet. I made my home overlooking the lake and noticed two button bucks across the way, slowly making their way around the lake to our area. I had never before seen a live buck or even a button buck, with their antlers covered in smooth velvet, except as carcasses strewn on the curb of the parkway, bloated or decapitated. These were shy, yet bold, their hooves leaving imprints in the mud, a story of their ambling days grazing grass and frolicking through the trees. Here, I lived among them, and among my new friends, this New York tramily, even if just for a night, laughing merrily around the fire while eating ramen. I needed companionship, and although their presence was temporary, I knew that something greater was coming.

I woke up to find my new friends gone, already headed out onto the trail, perhaps. They were in an awful hurry. Each had a deadline to adhere to: One had to go back to school, while the others had their own responsibilities. I had no ill will toward them. While I broke my camp down, I noticed two other tents, one green and one orange, two hundred feet from mine. It seemed like they were just waking up as well. The sky was hazy. The mist was starting, rising from the lake like steam does when water boils. Something told me that today was going to be different; it was a feeling I was learning to trust.

I boiled a quarter cup of water in my Toaks cooking pot. Today's breakfast would be instant butter grits fresh out the packet. I dug in with my long spoon and caught the two hikers out of the right corner of my eye. A young man appeared, his sleepy brown eyes turned upward like the eyes of the button buck I had watched the previous day. One button in his shirt was unhooked, opening at his throat, letting his coarse black chest hair peer through his shirt. A woman was with him. They smiled at me, not with their lips but with their eyes.

"Hey, we saw you from over the way and wanted to introduce ourselves."

The man reached out to brace himself on a tree and leaned into the sun's rays. "I need a little color these days. It's better than looking like Casper the ghost."

I laughed. "Hey, I'm Dragonsky. I'm just eating breakfast, getting ready to head out. What's your name?"

"The name's Captain Underpants—"

"And I'm Funghi," the young woman interrupted. "We love meeting other hikers. You hiking alone? Where you from? Where you headed to today?"

Her barrage of questions was the hiker norm, and I was as friendly and eager to answer them. I explained that I was from New Jersey, that I had been hiking solo for majority of the trail, and that I had fallen behind and lost my old tramily back at the New Jersey state line where they had gotten off.

Funghi's eyes dilated like a cat's.

"You're from New Jersey! Oh my god, can I say this . . . I was pleasantly surprised by how beautiful New Jersey was. I was not expecting that. May I ask you another question?"

Before I could answer, she swiftly went ahead.

"What is the night before Halloween called?"

"Mischief Night," I responded. This was the fourth time on trail that I had been asked that question; it had never occurred to me that the rest of the United States wasn't in on the messy festivities of egging houses and decorating them with ribbons of toilet tissue on that particular night. Another one of the many reasons I loved New Jersey.

"Yes, I knew it!" she screamed as Captain Underpants rolled his eyes playfully.

"I've got some packing to do, I'll join up with y'all in a bit," he said.

Funghi and I talked as I gobbled up my grits. Funghi had met Captain Underpants around Blood Mountain, in the first one hundred miles or so of the AT, and they had been hiking together since. As she chatted, I couldn't help but notice the shorts she was wearing, free of underwear, which I liked to do myself. To be completely free of societal standards of what women should look like or wear was empowering on trail. Our shared underarm hair was a testament to the fact that we embraced who we were, nature in its natural form unregulated by the male gaze. We were women united by our journey north and relieved to be in the company of feminine energy. I couldn't help but wonder if she was part of the rainbow, too. All of our talking had distracted me from packing up, and I started to get anxious. I wanted to hike with them, but I didn't know if they wanted to hike with me. And then, like magic, she granted my wish.

"Do you want to hike with us?"

I hesitated. "I am slow. . . . That's one of the reasons I have been hiking alone. Everyone seems to be doing twenty- to twenty-five-mile days, but I just wake up and see where the trail takes me. I have always been about the experience. So, if you don't mind, and I don't slow you down . . ."

"Well, what a match made in heaven! Captain and I have been feeling the same way lately. We took off fast and realized we really weren't having that much fun, making everything about miles and such. Like, when are we ever going to get to do this again? We might as well enjoy it. We won't mind hiking with you, Dragonsky. What do you say?"

"Sure, I'll give it a shot."

We met in front of the lake and took off. Our goal was to get to Bear Mountain in the next two days, where there was going to be friends and pizza, and I was invited.

I welcomed Bear Mountain with a hug of the white blazes. We were great friends through each season we had managed to see each other. I prepped my newfound friends for what was to come as if I were the official tour guide.

"Welcome to Bear Mountain! All of the City comes here to play, and by City, I mean New York City. Be prepared for drones, loud music, and large groups of—"

"Moogles," Funghi said.

"What are moogles?"

"Those are what we call the day hikers and those who climb mountains with no experience."

"Oh, okay! Well, large groups of moogles will be flocking all over the mountain and being rambunctious throughout this climb, so prepare well, thru-hikers!" I said.

Heading north up Bear Mountain lent me a new pair of eyes. I had only ever come from the south and stopped at its summit, never treading past that point. Large slabs of rock arched toward the sky, their surfaces sleek and soft like freshly ironed clothes. The dew hissed in the air like steam. It was pleasant and, most importantly, quiet, giving us a moment to embrace the silence and prepare for the next segment of our hike.

The City had a heartbeat, and it was carried here on the wind. I felt it brushing past my cheeks like a stroke of a butterfly's wings. With every step I took, the pounding of the beat amplified, the rhythm playing throughout the mountain. Today the City was alive among the trees, the band was marching in, and the concert-goers were rowdy. For the first time on the Appalachian Trail, I felt completely safe. There was nothing I feared on this mountain, for diversity thrived here. It was what New York City embodied and embraced—the heart of every human—while acknowledging the plight of each individual person and their cultural differences. People from all parts of the world lived alongside one another every day in the city, especially when shit hit the fan. Like on December 13, 2014, when I joined New Yorkers who came together to march after the brutal murder of Eric Garner by a white cop who held him in a choke hold over selling a loosie. On that day, I walked with people of all races, genders, ages, and sexual orientations, able-bodied or not, to take a stand for Black lives and let the world know that New York would not tolerate this shit happening here. The City was where I danced the night away at my first lesbian club, Henrietta Hudson, and where I was chosen as a background actress on a pilot with director Ava DuVernay. And today this City had come to me, unknowingly following the white blazes for a day hike of Bear Mountain.

We escaped the canopy of trees and the patchwork of boulders. The mountain gave way to views of the gorgeous blue mountains and of the City. Everything was good at this moment. A soft wind blew. I took in the present moment with my new friends, pausing in the sun's yellow glow.

After we got our fill of sunshine, we continued quickly, our bellies guiding us. At the bottom, a trail sign marked the miles to Katahdin and the Suffern–Bear Mountain Trail, the trail where I had been bestowed with my trail name. I posed for a quick picture, my legs clinging tight to the post of the sign, my shorts falling to my butt crack. At the base of the mountain, a carnival was strewn out across the grass. Bear Mountain State Park had all the latest tourist attractions—ice skating rink, lodge, and even a zoo, which the AT goes right through, marking the lowest point on the trail. It was a jarring scene for a thru-hiker who had spent the last few months in a green tunnel, high above the sleepy villages below. We followed the blazes around the lake, where there were tons of people taking advantage of the beautiful day as well. *Goodbye, safe haven; hello, fictional world.*

A man waved us over from across the lake; he must have spotted our thru-hiker attire. Funghi, Captain, and I made our way to a picnic table where three cardboard boxes lay stacked like pancakes. I pictured my first bite of real pizza made with real New York water. The key to a good crust is always in the water, and I missed that thin crunch, just enough mozzarella to not choke you or ignite the heart. Funghi and Captain introduced me to their friend, and they caught up on lost time while I feasted like a vulture. One slice, two, then three. As I ate, a foul smell crept under my nose.

Trash. There was trash everywhere. I stopped and looked in disgust. What the actual fuck was wrong with people? The turkeys were literally throwing their trash onto the ground. My shoulder blades tightened, and anger spread down my spine until I could no longer keep my cool. Something inside me wanted to bawl, to scream.

Looking at the moogles reminded me of a stark truth. I used to be one of them. As a kid, respecting nature was not what I was taught. Throwing trash on the sidewalks was something my mother had told me to do. She had never been exposed to nature; many inner-city Black folks aren't. Lack of access to the outdoors, transportation, and education about wilderness skills, coupled with intergenerational trauma—all were barriers. Knowing that our ancestors were lynched in the woods was word enough to stop many from going. In a moment of rage came a humbling thought: How could we expect others to respect nature if they were never taught how? They never learned the outdoor bible of *Leave no trace*. Neither had I, until I learned about the Appalachian Trail. It sucked to see the Earth trashed, but there was still hope that people could learn and change.

Just as the trail carried on, so did we. The Bear Mountain Bridge hovered over the Hudson below. A narrow sidewalk, just wide enough that we could walk in pairs, hugged the edge of the bridge, with a two-lane road with cars locked in traffic on my right. In front of us another giant awaited, Anthony's Nose. I'd picked it a few times and bypassed the view. The climb was steep but not terribly foreboding. While people dragged themselves back home to prepare for their workdays, I dragged myself up another mountain, as happy as I could be. There were now just the three of us who didn't owe the world anything. We wanted to go far together but not fast, touching the white blazes as we went, leaving the marks of our existence behind.

New York State was rocks, woods, and rebars—bars embedded in the rock to climb up or down on, like vertical monkey bars. What it lacked in scenery it made up for in deli stops along the way. Nothing could keep me from a proper hoagie, and I made it a habit to always buy two, one for now and one for packing to eat out on trail within the next two hours. Funghi and Captain stayed by my side through it all.

New York, just like PA, was a relief to get over and done with. When we made it, a new gateway opened. Spending 24/7/365 with my newfound friends allowed us to form deeper connections.

One day in Connecticut we stumbled upon Sages Ravine, a hidden gem of water and jungle. No one ever spoke or wrote of this place. I had researched the AT and binged YouTube videos, and not once was Sages Ravine spoken about. If there was a Grand Canyon of

New England, this would be it. Her waters rushed and tumbled over rocks, crashing down into giant whirlpools. There was something so enticing about the ravine that invited you to sit along the banks and drift into the mossy vegetation, to swim and be one with her waters. The trail was rugged and steep, slick and glossy. The near absence of light made for a dramatic scene, only adding to the allure. In the darkness, I sat there with my friends, and the light that shone through the canopy revealed them to me. We shared our stories, as tramilies do.

"Why did you both decide to hike the Appalachian Trail?" I asked.

Funghi was eager to go first.

"Well, I have known since I was ten that I wanted to thru-hike this trail. I served time in the military, and I've seen lots of things. I lost friends right in front of me. I hike for all my fallen sisters and brothers. I carry them with me in every step that I take."

I turned to Captain Underpants.

"Can we smoke a blunt before this?" he asked.

When he was ready, he began. "I hike because I never thought I could. I lost my parents when I was just seven years old and ended up in the foster system. If I survived that, I figured, what's two thousand one hundred and ninety-three miles? The stinging in my legs, the mosquitoes biting every inch of my damn body, the mud, the rain, and stupid PUDs—pointless ups and downs. Why climb a mountain to get within fifty feet of the summit just to make a sharp left and descend, or have the view obstructed by the freaking green tunnel? Well, that's the Appalachian Trail, honey . . . and it's fucking life. This trail exposes you like a cell under a microscope. Sunrises and sunsets aren't guaranteed; nothing is, especially trail magic."

I listened, rapt, giving him my full attention as he poured out his heart. "The AT, it can't break me. I'm already broken. I am trying to find myself again, to find a meaning to it all. Climbing mountains is funny. This trail is so easy. Maybe it's because I have experienced shit. But for reals, climbing mountains is nothing compared to the grief that I have lived with. I'm learning how resilient I am and how real humankind can be. Even on the nastiest days on the trail, I have found sunshine and rainbows in the hearts of other thru-hikers. It's like one big family out here. I could have given up many times in my life, you know? And there were so many moments when I knew I could end it all, but then this trail gave me hope—and it gave me both of you."

I could see why we had needed that blunt first. My heart said to him, *I see you.* I really did. I saw the pain and the perseverance. That guilt that he carried for all his life doubled his pack weight, yet he climbed mountains every day, rarely, if ever, complaining. In my life, I'd learned that hell existed on earth, and our souls could become trapped there. They never taught me *that* in church when they talked about hell. They mentioned the weeping and gnashing of teeth, but they forgot to ask, *What if that's someone's reality? What if mental illness is their ongoing hell, and what is the cost?*

Every day, people like us make a daring decision to continue our lives despite the pain and the voices that tell us, *Die, you're better off dead.* We, my Connecticut tramily, had made a commitment to the AT, to keep walking its trail just like we were walking the path of life. Up every mountain and down every valley, whether solo or together, all we knew was that we had to push forward toward the end of the trail and beyond.

This wasn't just any old walk in the woods. Katahdin wasn't the end. It couldn't be, not with the stories that we packed with us and carried on our backs.

WAXING CRESCENT

The battle I won at the bridge of the dam in Austin wouldn't be my last. A few weeks after, in February 2016, I found myself in the hospital, where I was admitted for a total of five days in a unit with twelve other patients suffering from depression and anxiety. We all came in dirty, looking to purge our souls of the muck that was trying to bury us. One moment we would be perfectly okay, and the next we were hollering and screaming. There were times I would be fine, until suddenly anxiety would punch me square in the face. Pacing up and down the hall each day with a breakdown was the norm, and nurses would come over and try to console me and offer me Ativan.

Luckily, the structure of a schedule helped me to find my feet.

Each day we were advised to participate in groups to help us learn coping skills, effective communication, and other techniques to better our mental states. The more one participated, the faster one would be released. Yoga was one of my favorites. Our instructor would bring in mats and lay them across the dayroom like they used to do in preschool. We would start with a stretch followed by downward dog, then we would pick up the beat and do cardio workouts such as jumping jacks. I had always thought yoga was just a bunch of stretches, but I was completely wrong. Yoga was the most intense and sweaty exercise of them all.

My absolute favorite activity was "visiting time," scheduled between four and six p.m. every day. Parents, friends, and extended family would come in a few times a week to visit their loved ones and offer much-needed support. Nearly every day I had Pepper, friends from AmeriCorps, or a few people from the church come and spend their evenings after work with me. Many times I felt disgusting, ashamed, and embarrassed that those I loved could see me at such a crippling point in my life. I was dressed in blue scrubs or sweatpants and shoes without laces and marked with a hospital band. I felt like a slave to a system that branded me wherever I went. My files were in the hands of staff, doctors, and therapists who could write whatever they wanted about me, and there was no way I could access them. I thought that I was a sick individual who had succumbed to her illness rather than the strong Black woman I had been raised to be. But my loved ones didn't give a rat's ass about that. They only cared about my safety and my life. They saw me in all my strength instead of my flaws and weaknesses. As each day droned on, I began to feel like they were walking right beside me.

Eventually, the light began to shine in, and after five days with proper medication and therapy, I was released to intensive outpatient for the next seven weeks. Four times a week at dawn, I drove on Interstate 35 across town to attend meetings where we'd share our experiences with the group and learn strategies for how to manage our emotions, recognize and understand our triggers, and develop coping skills. Knowing our boundaries and asserting ourselves was critical for many of us with mental health disorders, unseen illnesses that enabled us to be taken advantage of and given no sympathy in society.

At the end of the seven weeks, the group leader congratulated me. Then, as always with a graduate, he posed the question "Are you ready?"

That question felt like a test as well as an observation. I felt that it was meant to make me question my very sanity and the ability to survive without the support of regular meetings. What is "ready"? To live with mental illness, have a crisis, be placed into such a structured setting like a hospital or outpatient facility, and then suddenly released into a society that deems you "other" and stigmatizes you is startling. Going back to work, being asked by nosy coworkers what happened, and having to go through the motions of working while saving face or trying to avoid an episode is purely exhausting. Having to come back to reality is harsh.

No, I wasn't ready. But for the sake of answering his question, I simply nodded and said, "Yes."

I had to be. I was feeling as strong as an ox and almost back to my normal self. My friends were waiting, and I knew they would be ecstatic to have me back. With all the courage in my heart, I walked out of IOP and told myself I would never end up back there if I could help it.

But how do you tame a beast you cannot cage? Mental illness cannot be cured, only treated.

My new fire fueled me to leave AmeriCorps and follow my dreams of being a veterinarian technician. Emancipet, a low-cost vaccine and spay-and-neuter clinic, gave me the stepping stones to success over the next two years. Litters of vivacious, restless, and adorable puppies came through our office frequently. Ten-hour shifts were expected four days a week, with three off days for regaining the countless amounts of energy exhausted by lifting and wrestling the animals. Patients were in abundance and breaks were scarce, which increased tension and stress among the staff. But staying busy did wonders for my mental health, as I barely had any time to be alone with the monsters inside my head. It was a relief to have them muzzled and frail.

As my mental disorders slept like a dormant volcano, my physical health started to show signs of wear. Handling and struggling with feral cats and dogs of all sizes ended up being detrimental to my thoracic spine, but it was the price I paid for the love of saving animals. Around this time, I also rescued a sweet black-and-tan Australian Kelpie mix puppy whom I named Meraxes after a dragon from the mind of George R.R. Martin. Meraxes became my guardian angel. Whenever my thoughts drifted to dark places, whenever I thought of death and of ending the pain and suffering so I wouldn't be a burden to others, the other part of me flashed to my helpless eight-pound puppy back home who had just defeated parvovirus, giardia, and getting spayed. Did Meraxes love me? How would she feel if I was gone? Meraxes never faltered. No matter how sick she was, she continued to prance around the house and tug at me to play with her. When I was down, she brought me toys, and she lay in my lap. She never gave up.

Neither could I.

But as surely as the moon waxes and wanes, so does mental illness. Medication and therapy are great . . . until they aren't. Relapse is always lurking in the shadows, waiting for a stressful event or failure in medication to show itself once more.

I dabbled in jobs, eventually broke up with Pepper, found a new roommate, and started life again in East Austin. Then the monsters returned for another vicious cycle in the spring of 2018. Depression crept in through the back door without a sound, sticking its ghastly hand into my brain, toying with it as if it were a chemistry experiment. I felt worthless and pathetic after my breakup with Pepper. I engaged in self-destructive behaviors that were out of my character. Vivid nightmares came to me, of tornadoes spawning multiple tornadoes while I sheltered in a basement with my aunt as the town around us was torn to shreds by winds of two hundred miles per hour. Sleep deprivation affected my mood, and the will to live slowly faded out, as a rainbow gradually does after a rainstorm.

For the first time in my life, I became truly homeless when I was evicted from the apartment I shared with two roommates. I was left to fend for myself while mentally ill, a road I had never been on before. Driving around Austin, I saw tents lined up beneath the shadows of Interstate 35. Urine as pungent as a cat's marked the territory of the poor; it was enough to keep anyone at bay. Some of the people I saw stood up straight while others were bent over as if someone had rammed them in the torso with a pickup truck. Many of them were mentally ill, screaming to themselves in babbles that neither a baby nor a priest would comprehend. I had never wanted to be *them*. I never thought I would be exactly in their shoes, with the only difference being that I had my car to sleep in.

I had a single black garbage bag that contained all my belongings; the other items that did not fit in the bag were either dumped or sold. Years of clothing that I had become accustomed to and trinkets that I had collected were gone. The purple Nintendo GameCube my aunt had given me one Christmas was now an object I had to sell for survival. These were reminders of my childhood, my life without limitations, and my life with love and security, and I would never get them back. All I had left were memories, and the objects had borne more of that weight than I expected.

The streets were my new home, and I needed a safe place where I could sleep in my car and not be harassed. Walmart was a viable option, as I had seen cars and campers parked overnight on many occasions. At night, homeless folks living on the streets would hang out in the Walmart parking lot, scurrying for shelter beneath the trees, testing their loitering skills. Fear played with my mind at night, as I was worried about other homeless people approaching me in my car, but luckily I had Meraxes and a Taser gifted to me from a friend who knew my situation. With Meraxes and the Taser, sleeping in the car at night wasn't so bad—until the morning.

Dawn was a sinister friend. The heat she brought was unbearable, especially for a dog. Meraxes panted heavily, drenching my car seat in dog saliva. I knew that the situation could be deadly for my dog, and I wasn't ready to lose her. With any money I had left over during the week, I gave my dog temporary shelter with strangers I had never met before. Kind people opened their homes to her, and I had no right to complain. Even knowing she stayed in a flea-infested home was a much more comfortable thought than her dying of heatstroke in the back seat of my car. All we had was each other now; we were each other's lifelines.

Living on the streets took a serious toll on my mental health and ability to get proper mental health care. Without anyone to help me, and drained of resources, I finally had no choice but to take myself to Psychiatric Emergency Services.

Going to PES voluntarily was generally, if not always, better than going involuntarily. Involuntary admission could result in longer hospital stays, as when I was a child, with the inability to sign yourself out. In those instances, you were typically led in by the police because of a crisis situation. I hated that. Cops scared me, as they continued to slaughter Black and Brown bodies with no regard for human life. I did not want to be a Deborah Danner or an Eleanor Bumpurs.

Deborah Danner, a New Yorker, was sixty-six and suffered from schizophrenia. A neighbor called the cops on her to report that she was emotionally disturbed, and in due time the cops came. Apparently, the news reported, she had come at the cop with a bat, and the cop shot her in the torso not once but twice. She lay dead as her sister watched in horror. Eleanor Bumpurs was similarly shot dead after a psychiatrist deemed it necessary to have Eleanor committed for her mental illness. The police were called to evict Eleanor and get her hospitalized—but instead, she never left her apartment alive.

Through scenario after scenario, my brain scrambled for air as it buried itself in anxiety. *Is this the right choice? Will they steal my cells like Henrietta Lacks, without the world knowing for years? Will they inject me with infectious diseases like they did at Tuskegee, when hundreds of men were used in Syphilis experiments with no consent and received no medication, even when it became available. And they did this for decades.* This was Texas; anything could happen. Unfortunately, I had no other option. When you have to choose between a bad-case scenario and a worst-case scenario, what do you do? I was evaluated at PES and eventually sent to a place called the Den, which ended up being one of the biggest regrets of my life.

The center itself was pristine and brand new. There were eight rooms, each containing two patients of the same sex. Bright lights illuminated the halls and were to remain on all night long. Sufficient sleep was nearly impossible for my roommate and me; we both suffered from insomnia. Rooms were rarely cleaned, and when they were, they had a great idea to shampoo the carpet at night before we went to bed. Strong chemical odors similar to Windex and bleach on steroids immersed the room in their poison, and my roommate, an older Italian woman who had breathing issues, suffered for it. There was no mercy as she wheezed and coughed, forcing her to leave the room or suffer the physical consequences. Bathrooms were housed in our rooms, but showers were communal and cleaned once a week. I always made sure to wear my tacky pink flamingo flip-flops that had AUSTIN, TX engraved on them to avoid the germs that thrived merrily on the shower floor. The dining room consisted of six round tables, two water fountains, and a handwashing station that was always clogged with leftover food. Monopoly and Connect Four lay on the sleek baby-blue rectangular table that sat in the center of the dayroom surrounded by sofas and chairs of all sorts. It was a small room with translucent windows, a navy-blue rug, and a shit ton of VCR cassettes and DVDs.

Case managers worked in a secluded section of the building, only accessible with a special key they had. Most staff were as cold as the rooms themselves. They rarely smiled or made eye contact, making me feel as if I were invisible. Every pack has an alpha, and the alpha at the Den demanded to be obeyed. Her presence was unwelcoming and lacking emotion. Manipulation and unethical behavior were her cup of tea in the morning, and even her employees quivered behind their desks when she walked by. She was punitive, constantly enforcing rules that held no merit. Soap was not to be given out anymore, as we "left cups of soap in the bathroom." Soap wasn't the only item she took away; shampoo and food accommodations were also under her control. Dairy was never something my stomach agreed with, and when I broached the topic, she looked at me with disgust, like I was bullshitting her.

"You're not allergic. . . . You don't have any dietary restrictions!"

PES was built for those who didn't have the privilege of wealth; we were the poor, the uninsured, and the undeserving who had to endure being ignored and treated less than because we were underprivileged. As a human and an empath, and as someone who too many times had had my pleas and cries invalidated by doctors and psychiatrists because I was a Black woman, I shared the other patients' pain. Many were very ill and could not advocate for themselves. They were either mute or their words were disregarded as crazy talk.

Situations always seemed to arise and escalate quickly without warning. One night a fire drill was conducted about two hours after we had all been given our sedative nighttime medications. Flashing lights danced like strobes as the alarm screamed with all of its might, awakening the deepest of sleepers. Staff began pounding their fists on our heavy metal doors.

"Fire drill, let's go! Get up!"

I went out into the hallway where other patients had gathered, just as confused as I was. The staff came for Chris last, a patient who wasn't about to put up with nobody's shit. Yelling erupted from his bedroom, blistering fury accompanying his words. "I'M NOT GOING!" He embodied the power of Krakatoa, the walls trembling around him. He stood his ground until his strength could endure no more, and then he joined us in the parking lot. Streetlights shimmered in the shadows of the night. We stood apart from the staff who had pulled this shit on us. The alpha appeared.

"Looks like we might have to do this fire drill again tomorrow night, since some of y'all didn't want to get up."

I was truly astonished that someone could be such a bitch as to put vulnerable people at risk, and for what?

The patients became rowdy and vocal.

"I'm going to report you to the board!" yelled Chris. "This isn't right! You cannot do this to people! I am writing to them! This is bullshit. Fuck this shit!"

He was ready to attack. He had been hurt in the drill when he slipped and fell because his medication caused drowsiness and dizziness. Meanwhile, the staff were sitting around with their thumbs up their asses. Empathy was absent in a profession that necessitated it. Chris ultimately refused medical attention and gave the staff hell. I approved; I hated that place. We were humans, too, who had to live with illnesses that were not physically noticeable. We could only take so much.

One day, I broke, and I paid the price for a bold lie.

Every day you were allowed to leave the building for three hours to do whatever you pleased. I still had a job at a grocery store and had to maintain it to provide for Meraxes, who was being housed by a coworker. But one day I forgot to ask for permission to go to work. All requests had to be written the night before and approved for the morning. Desperate for money and to keep my job, I forged a signature. The staff found out. They explained that I had broken the rules and that they were "going to kick me out."

Upset, I yelled, "How do you kick someone out of the mental hospital when you have no idea what the state of their mental condition is? What if I was suicidal?"

That was the straw that broke the camel's back, and they called the police. The next thing I knew, animal control showed up. They were coming for Meraxes. Meraxes immediately sensed what was about to occur. Her hair stood straight up on her haunches. Terrified, she pulled back with all her strength to escape the noose that reached for her at the end of a thick five-foot handle. Our eyes connected as she pleaded and cowered for me to set her free from the monster who would return her to the pound where her life had started. Her tail found shelter as she tucked it firmly between her muscular thighs while I looked on in horror. The officer managed to get her into the cold gray van and locked her in a cell. I glanced once more into her melancholy eyes as the rusted metal handcuffs grasped my wrists and my arms were put behind my back. Mental illness was not a crime, and yet it was protocol to be handcuffed as a criminal for the safety of both parties.

As the pound truck pulled away, I felt my body hit the ground.

"I—want my dog! She's my dog! She is my dog. Someone do something!"

Gasping and crying. I screamed once more.

"PLEASE DON'T TAKE MY DOG . . . PLEASE DON'T TAKE . . . PLEASE!"

A female cop stood nearby with her hair in a tight ponytail, not a single hair straying from the bunch. She glanced at me and walked over.

"She will be fine. You can get her when you get better."

But I wasn't sick to the point that my dog had to be taken away from me. She was not a criminal, and I had not committed a crime, but we were both being punished. They spoke in twisted tongues, obscuring the truth. My lifeline had literally been pried from my warm hands. Being separated from my dog threw me into a deep sadness, one that could not be altered by the rays of the sun or comforted by the light of the moon. It was as if she had died, but this actually felt worse than death. Against my will, I was thrown in the back seat of the hideous patrol car. I had only taken this ride once before, once when I was younger and I didn't come home before the streetlights were on, and my grandma called the cops. Black metal bars lined each window, leaving cracks to peep through to see the free world around you. The seat was as hard as a boulder. Comfort is not a factor in the manufacturing of law enforcement patrol cars, but then again, neither is it for the jails and prisons in America. Inside the car, a thick, hard plastic screen separated those in power from the powerless. Spit, feces, and urine had probably been splattered on that screen by hundreds of humans demanding that they be set free. I could understand why now. Texas had failed me for the final time. Now I fully understood that not everything in Texas was bigger and better. I had an even more pressing reason to leave.

But first, I was admitted to a new hospital called City Lake.

Baby-blue paint gave the frigid room a faint glow in the dreary darkness. Nurses walked frantically back and forth on the hardwood floors, their mission to collect vital signs and psychiatric information. In front of each wall sat a stained forest-green couch occupied by five other patients eagerly awaiting their turn to meet with the medical doctor before heading up to our floor. Time seemed to come to a complete halt, but all we had was time.

"We all come from beautiful broken nests," an older white man who sat to the left of me said. He had already been hospitalized multiple times due to bipolar disorder.

Melody, a young woman in her early twenties, had very pale skin, as if she never saw the light of the sun. Her vision seemed obstructed by the weight of the yellow glasses that slid down her nose. A rectangular table decorated with four sheets of printer paper and two crayons rested between us, and this she enjoyed very much. She paced back and forth, organizing everything in sight. The blue crayon came before the green crayon but could not be within five inches of the white paper. Nothing was permitted to touch, including the food we were served. Long strands of al dente spaghetti doused in a red sauce sat in the left corner of a teal tray with a piece of garlic bread that was inadvertently marred by a hint of red no bigger than the tip of a ballpoint pen. Someone was going to have to answer for the evil acts of impurity committed against Melody, and she let it be known.

"Why is my sauce touching my bread? Oh man . . . it's ruined. The food cannot touch! My food is touch—"

"Melody, dear, it's okay, just rip it off or don't eat it at all, you already know the drill," said one of the nurses.

She settled down and counted her losses. The bread had to go, but at least there were Oreos. I gave Melody my Oreos because I for sure wasn't going to eat them. I had had enough Oreos in my childhood.

"What's your name?" came her nearly silent whisper.

"Huh?"

"What's your name?" Melody repeated.

"My name is Shilletha."

"Shilletha, hmmm . . ."

She pondered as if she were given a math equation to solve for X. Silence soon followed, and she simply walked away from the conversation. Seconds later I saw her nestled in the fetal position on one long green couch. Hibernation had come early as she fell into a deep slumber, oblivious to the screams of distressed patients in the unit around the corner. While she slept peacefully, images of home floated through my mind. Thin-crust pizza with rustic tomato sauce, chewy bagels made just right, and the familiar hint of sea salt blowing inland from the ocean sent me into bliss. New Jersey was 1,759 miles from me, and here in Austin, I felt so lonely and empty. Lost in a sea of memories, I self-soothed as I relived a snowball fight on the Atlantic City boardwalk with old friends. What the fuck was I doing in Texas, home to the worst mental health care in the country? I needed to get out. I decided that after my seventy-two-hour hold at the psychiatric hospital, I would get my dog and head back to where I knew I would have support—New Jersey.

"Shilletha Curtis?" a woman yelled out from around the corner.

I stood up, careful not to wake the sleeping beauty. I was taken into a small ten-by-ten room with mint-green walls. I was stripped down, my body searched from head to toe by two middle-aged female nurses to check for scars from self-harm and other small physical abnormalities. I was asked the usual questions, and I explained my situation to the nurses and that there was nothing wrong with me. Homelessness had sparked desperation in me, and having a roof over my head was better than being in my car, but then I had broken the rules at the Den because I had to have money to support my dog and me. They weren't really buying my story, but they said they would hold me for seventy-two hours and evaluate me then. Acting out wasn't an option anymore; my best bet was to fake it until I made it, for the sake of getting Meraxes back and getting the hell back to New Jersey.

Moments later, I was in the elevator that led to our unit. At least I would be with the somewhat normal crowd and not on the floor of "high elopement," where people truly lost their shit. In our unit, I met an eighteen-year-old girl named Sarai. During intake, they had deemed her "high risk" because she had attempted to end her life through a dangerous method, and they placed her in the "high elopement unit" before transferring her here. Sarai had stories to tell for days that scared every single one of us who listened in with eager ears about what went down in the other unit.

"There were two people taking their heads and smashing them into each other, like BAM BAM! Yo, that shit was wild, I ain't never seen any shit like that. And then, wait, listen, listen! There was another patient who got mad over his dinner not having dessert, and he took the table and threw it. That shit was the craziest shit I have ever seen!"

Empathy swelled in my heart for Sarai. I felt equally bad for the patients who were so ill that they could not function on a level that would guarantee them a good quality of life. The majority of the patients in my unit struggled with depression, anxiety, and borderline personality disorder, while the patients on the other floor were so blind to their illnesses that they probably had no awareness of how sick they had become. I thought about their families and friends, and the lives they had or didn't have because of the deep wounds of mental illness. A heavy bag sat on my back, filled with the guilt I had for feeling grateful that I didn't need as much support and aware of my illnesses.

I had heard through the grapevine that City Lake was notorious for locking patients out of their rooms and making them participate in groups even if they didn't want to. Being forced to do something against my will was not my cup of tea. My whole life I had been a rebel, and not having the choice to say no reminded me of all the sexual trauma in my past. Losing the power to choose felt like bondage and slavery. But I also knew that participating in a group was paramount to being released from the cage that I was bound in, and so I went every day.

It was a pleasant surprise. The staff was diverse and consisted of predominantly Black folks who were down to earth and real with the patients on the unit. Everyone was especially kind to me, including my roommate, who dealt with anorexia. Her blue scrubs hung off of her arms and legs to hide the bones that were desperately screaming for nourishment. Hunger could not be fended off. She was mostly silent, but her facial expressions were bold and spoke of all the mystery she concealed. The battle with her illness had taken its toll, but I was glad that she was finally getting help and relief in the hospital; hell, I was glad that all of us on the unit were reaching out for help and continuing to fight for our lives when our illnesses wanted nothing but to lay us in our early graves. Some wished for death as

I had, but I wasn't ready to give in. Something bigger was coming.

Three days later, I met with the psychiatrist and received a clean bill of health for departure into the world of fiction and social constructs once again. Leaving was bittersweet; it always was. The allure of freedom was strong but came with a lack of the structure, constant surveillance, and support that I had in the hospital. It was as if I were learning to ride a bike again without the training wheels, only the lesson was becoming a semi-functioning human in a world where mental illness was widely misunderstood. There would be no one to make sure I had eaten a meal or who would hold me accountable for taking my medications that day. It would just be Meraxes and me, but we would get through it together.

My friend Greg picked me up at noon and brought me back to PES to retrieve my Nissan. With my keys and a heavy foot, I slammed down the gas pedal and pushed forward. We were off to the animal shelter to grab my dog. Sweat doused me as if it were a scorching summer day and my breath began to pick up. Every nerve in my body suddenly lit up with electricity as thoughts of reuniting with my dog filled my heart with love and memories. It felt as if the Earth rotated on its axis a full two times during the ten-minute ride, but then I saw the sign of the animal shelter. Aggressively, I whipped my car into the parking spot as if I were about to pull off a heist. There was no time to waste as I swung the glass doors open and ran up to the young woman at the counter.

"Hello! My name is Shilletha Curtis, and my dog, Meraxes, got taken in three days ago. I am here to pick her up. Please tell me she's—"

"What did you say your name was again?" the woman interrupted.

"Shilletha Curtis."

"Okay, Shilletha, give us a few minutes, and we will have her out for you."

"Yes!" I nearly climbed over the desk and onto the frightened, frail woman I had been shouting at.

Minutes later, a black-and-tan dog came out with her happy tail erect in the air like an antenna.

"OH, MY BABY! THANK YOU, THANK YOU!" I shrieked.

What Meraxes gave me in love could never be tainted by the hands of humans. She was loyal and loving, an angel plated in velvet fur with a bark that could make a grown man cower in the night. We had braved the strong tides in high seas, danced under the light of the waning crescent, and glanced at the stars and how they shone for us, millions of light-years away. Even stars died, but their light still shone, thousands of years later. I had died many times, but my light never waned, even if it was concealed under the mask of mental illness. Now it was time for the mask to be removed. It was time to fight for Meraxes.

It was time to save my life.

Day and night, I called shelters, the church, or really whoever would hear me out and begged for help. Shame riddled me. I had labored for everything I had gotten and achieved throughout my resilient life, but explaining my mental illness or traumatic history to strangers made me feel little. A society that does nothing to stop the shame and stigma of blaming women for rape made me think twice about telling my story. But then Sharoness, a dear friend I had first met back in my Austin church choir, reached out to me and saved me. Our friendship had always been magnetic, from day one. We both had supernatural gifts that brought us together: I was a lightworker, chosen to bring humanity and peace to the world. I could sense but not see energies from other realms, both good and bad. Meanwhile, Sharoness was a witch who could cast spells and who helped Earth-trapped souls cross over to other realms and even sent sprits for protection. We both laughed at the notion of the church's hell, knowing that our spiritual gifts revealed much more in the grand scheme of the universe and the afterlife, and we soon vacated the church as our gifts were deemed witchcraft.

Sharoness was the only soul who helped me during this time. With Sharoness, I felt no shame as she listened to my story. Her words were gentle and warmhearted as she offered me her house as a place to stay while she gathered money to send me home to New Jersey and to fix my car. She bargained with her landlord, who graciously allowed Meraxes to stay, too. My heart galloped.

I was thankful for finally having shelter over my head, but comfort was a concept that was still foreign to me. To be comfortable when depression and abuse had shit on me and nearly washed me away was scary. I started to develop a mindset that when things went well, they could never stay good because something bad was bound to happen.

For two weeks, I stayed with my friend, delivering groceries for Instacart during the day and spending time with my dog at night. Then the final day came. My skin crawled to get the hell out of Texas, but I was also leaving Sharoness, my sister. I had always wanted a sister, even though I had a distant biological one. Sharoness fit the sister box. Sisters are inseparable. Sometimes they fight, but they have an unbreakable bond that only they can understand. We hugged tightly, knowing that we would remain sisters forevermore in the other realms.

Saying goodbye was not easy, but a new life was waiting for me in New Jersey. Getting into my car once more, I packed up what few things I had, buckled Meraxes in, and put my foot to the gas pedal and never looked back. Austin, Texas, was now a distant memory in my rearview mirror. It was time for metamorphosis.

Driving halfway across the country, I knew that everything would be okay. Life was a labyrinth. Mental illness had stolen my opportunities, friendships, and income and led me to poverty. The snowball never stopped rolling down the hill. But although I was lost, at least I was somewhere. Being lost was temporary, and I knew someday that something would call me home. And it did, even if "home" wasn't the singular place I had always expected. If I had not hit rock bottom, perhaps I would have never left Austin. Perhaps I would have never found my true purpose. And when you find your destiny, everything falls into place, and the people you need will show up and help you along the way. How could I have predicted what would lie in store for me over the next few years, how a chance meeting with a man on a mountain trail would send me to walk across the country through fourteen states?

As nighttime fell, I gazed up toward the heavens. There was no trace of the moon. A new cycle was beginning.

WHITE MOUNTAINS, NEW HAMPSHIRE

For months, I wondered when my "trail legs" would come in. After all, I had recently summited Mount Greylock in Massachusetts, Mount Killington in Vermont, and other giants whose long, tedious climbs pushed my body to near exhaustion. At a certain point, every thru-hiker can run up a mountain, their legs now strong pillars of muscle, conditioned after months of climbing. And when I crossed the state line from Vermont into New Hampshire, it was like a light switch was powered on. I inhaled deep breaths, my lungs expanding like helium balloons. I was no longer struggling every ten minutes for oxygen and to relieve the cramping in my sides. Instead, I was Goliath standing on the head of the giants, a young woman with dreads in a state that thousands of hikers didn't make it to. Only 20 percent of people who attempt the Appalachian Trail successfully complete it, and suddenly, in New Hampshire, I knew that I would be one of them. I was approaching mile 1756, Hanover, New Hampshire, about 450 miles from Katahdin.

It was such a good day that I danced right past the VT/NH engraving on the marble bridge. I was high on life, clicking my trekking poles together and singing my favorite song, "Stubborn Love" by the Lumineers. The trail veered out of the safety of the woods and into the core of the town. After a two-mile road walk, I found myself in the heart of Dartmouth University. The streets were bustling. I waved to people with a Ronald McDonald smile on my face as they stared back silently, enclosed in their containers. I watched the locals eagerly, waiting for them to offer me hot dogs, pizza, anything, before I realized that very few people here were familiar with AT thru-hikers. My face flushed with warmth as I collected myself with shaky hands and clenched fists. Hanover was a hard contrast to my life in the woods. Day after day, the forest was my universe, and imagining anything other was delusion. Now, busy streets, car motors, and the rat race of society were back at my forefront.

Funghi and Captain had arrived in Hanover earlier than me, having booked it to town. I found them at the Base Camp Café, a restaurant that served Himalayan dishes, arguably the best town food I had ever had on trail. I ordered shrimp tarkari, a dish I had never heard of, while Funghi and Captain played it safe by ordering chicken momos, steamed dumplings. Once we had our fill, we hiked back across town to our lodging for the night, a place called Hanover

Adventure Tours, where hikers could also rent electric bikes or tubes to float down the river. We checked into the center and got the grand tour of the showers, bunk rooms, and common areas.

Funghi and Captain vanished behind the walls of the room they had booked together while I explored. Board games lay scattered on a table, and a small shop sold the cutest yellow-and-black dress I'd ever seen—it was love at first sight. I snatched it and ran into the shower to change. When I emerged, I ripped the hiker runway with a Batman dress, its frilly tutu bottom as vibrant as a bee. With the day still young, I took advantage of what the adventure center had to offer. Electric bikes and tubing were at my disposal, and for a discounted hiker rate, how could I resist? I decided I would take a double zero to experience Hanover; miles could wait. That night, I took the town by storm on a rented electric bike with two hikers I had met. Zooming by cars, wearing my Batman dress, I felt like a superhero. When the night came to an end, I tumbled into my bunk, tipsy and content, blissfully unaware of what would happen the next morning.

The sun rose like she always did. The clock read eight a.m., and my lids hung low but my head was high. Hearing movement outside in the common room, I stumbled to my feet to investigate.

Funghi and Captain were outside, their packs packed and ready to go. What the fuck? We hadn't discussed this. The wind shifted. The morning sun gave way to fog clouds as anxiety rolled in. *Breathe*, I told myself. *Let's get to the bottom of this.*

"What's going on, guys?" I asked.

Their eyes met mine. Funghi played with a strand of her hair as Captain spoke.

"So, Funghi and I have a change in plans. Funghi wants to summit Katahdin on her birthday, the first of October. It is very dear to her, and we both discussed it."

They watched as I processed their words. The first of October was only a short while away.

"I wish we had been able to discuss it as a tramily. I am sorry. You are welcome to join, but we are leaving today instead of tomorrow. We can hike really slow so that you can try to catch up with us."

The ground I stood on suddenly felt precarious. I was terrified that any gust of wind would bring me to my knees. *How can they just leave me behind?* Here they were saying these words as if we hadn't just walked a couple hundred miles together, laughing, crying, and drinking together. It was as if they were speaking a language that I could not understand. But I did. I knew what this meant for me. We had talked about summiting together, but that was then, and this was now. Nature changed constantly, and so did the bonds I held on to.

Despite my heart breaking at the news, deep down I wasn't surprised. My childhood was a mirror to everything in my life, and people going and coming, arriving and leaving, wasn't anything new. Everything in life was temporary except the mountains. From day one I had set out to thru-hike the Appalachian Trail alone, and I knew that those I had met and hiked with along the way would never leave me permanently. Losing and gaining tramily gave me a new perspective on life: that family is chosen, that blood isn't always thicker than water. Each tramily taught me something valuable: Turtle and the kids showed me that I wasn't alone as a Black woman on trail, while Funghi and Captain showed me it was okay to be vulnerable. Opening ourselves to one another taught me that you truly never know what anyone is going through, and that kindness is the key to love, acceptance, and understanding. The friendships I made on the Appalachian Trail were forever, and the trail had always provided people who looked out for me in the moments I most needed support. Just like my aunt had said.

I said my final goodbyes. I walked up to them, arms out for a hug, and we embraced. It was the proper thing to do. Then I backed up, hands in my pockets. The tears streamed down my face, but I barely noticed them. My eyes were focused on their backs and the closing of the door. I cried and I cried and I cried, the ghosts of them still lingering in the room. The walls that contained me were my new prison, and I was unable to leave until three days later.

Even with acceptance came the very real human emotion of grief. In the days and weeks that followed, depression punched me in the face like a bully on the playground after school. Maintaining my mileage became burdensome, and I crumbled from fifteen down to three miles a day as my mind went astray with the whys and hows of what had happened. Smoke poured from my heart into the air, the acrid scent of bitterness filling my soul. But depression didn't win. Nature stood still as the last nostalgic warmth of summer eased into the sweet chill of September. Soon the mountains would be aflame, a wildfire of melodramatic red and auburn leaves. As I awoke into my new reality, I breathed in the sacred air of the White Mountains, and I breathed out the darkness that had tried to infiltrate.

Seven months of memories, experiences, and challenges had prepared me to stand at the base of the 4,800-foot Mount Moosilauke, the first climb in the Whites and one deemed by thru-hikers to be incredibly difficult. Below the mighty mountain is a town called Glencliff, where the Hikers Welcome Hostel awaited me. Behind the two bunkhouses, three tent spaces were available, which I gladly took advantage of. Touching the floors or tables inside the hostel made me want to scrub my skin ferociously with a pumice stone. Brown stains saturated the white mattresses, while the floors were so dark that I couldn't tell what color the carpet was. Hair, dirt, and filth lingered in the air. I took a whiff of the atmosphere, my nostrils flaring. *Yup, now that's a smell. Nursing home, ten-day-old wet socks, and man's underarm funk.*

Unlike me, other thru-hikers weren't so concerned about the interior design, and plenty filled up the bunks. The hostel offered slackpacking for Mount Moosilauke, and I got together with a few hikers to jump in on a car ride to save money. We'd be at the trailhead the next morning at seven a.m. and would end up back at the hostel at night, where our gear stayed. When the golden rays were still young the next day, I sprang up with intention. The weather was forecast to turn nasty swiftly after twelve, and every second counted. Both northbound or southbound on Moosilauke were ordinarily viable options, but judging by word of mouth that many hikers going north had fallen and needed to be helicoptered out because of the slippery conditions, I decided southbound was the safest choice. I started my ascent with a daypack carrying a headlamp, water filter, bladder, raincoat, an extra base layer top, and a boatload of snacks. It was time to send it.

Mighty Moosilauke sprinkled her fairy dust on me, and I immediately fell head over heels in love with her. She meant business. Her ascent was treacherous in the most beautiful way, gaining nearly one thousand feet (about 304.8 meters) per mile. The towering trees, steep moist rocks, and sinister roots and rebars kept my blood pumping, while the nearby creek supplied my endless thirst for water. Her rock-speckled summit was windswept, washed in sunlight, fully exposed, and brilliantly panoramic. In the distance, menacing clouds formed in lines like armies ready for battle. I glimpsed the blue sky above me, basking in what little light was left before a faint rumble of thunder nudged me on. Quickly, I descended and arrived back at the hostel, settling into bed just as lightning began to strike the earth.

That was only a taste of what I would later endure alone, entering a land known for the world's worst weather. In other states, I could afford to be oblivious to the weather; not so here. I ascended higher than I ever had, looking out over the tops of trees, across the great kingdom of mountains that stretched on for miles. I had hiked through a wooded aisle from Georgia to Vermont, guarded by the canopies of the trees. But now the green tunnel of entangled webs of rhododendron and mountain laurel had vanished. There were new watchers now, high upon the ridges in this sacred land of the White Mountains. I walked on a winding road that led straight into the heavens, spaces the Appalachian Trail had kept secret for nearly twelve states. High above the alpine zone, in this pristine utopia, I traversed rough terrain and past towers of cairns consisting of softball-sized boulders.

Months ago, I was merely a caterpillar wriggling down the trail, so very hungry for love, acceptance, and belonging, feeding on any leaf I could find. The green tunnel, my safe cocoon, had protected, nourished, and concealed me as I underwent metamorphosis. But now my old shell was no more, and from that new life came.

Dragonsky spread her wings on the colossal Franconia Ridge, a trail that soared high above the earth. Two borders of stacked stones lined the trail, which was the norm in the Whites above the tree line to guide hikers along the trail when the fog made it invisible. Step by arduous step, I danced up the mountain alongside an older thru-hiker.

"It must be nice to be young and have all that energy," he scoffed.

His slothlike pace was meticulous and precise; his rugged pack carried life-saving equipment. Two one-liter water bottles filled his pack pockets on both sides, and inside was a water bladder attached to a hose and insulin. He was diabetic and one determined motherfucker. As he vanished behind me, my pace took on its own rhythm, a vibe, a song that only I knew. Nothing hurt anymore, not my legs, back, or neck. All that remained was an all-encompassing love, growing stronger the farther I got from the strongholds of society.

When I reached the top among the slumbering giants, I, too, slumbered at Little Haystack Mountain. Under the night sky came a blanket of pearls, ablaze in the celestial fabric of eternity. The stars were always there, but the darkness revealed their light, their true beauty, I told myself. Ecstatic, I gave up my shelter and committed myself to the raw earth; I'd be one with the universe tonight.

The next morning, my breath dissolved the speckles of frost clinging to my bag.

"Is this real?" I asked myself as I took in the view.

The White Mountains are not like other spaces; they are alive. Trees were caught in a violent tussle between wind and earth. The mountain path continued amid the trees, hugging the curves of the land. High up on this ridge, I felt untouchable. I had arrived at my haven, an island of mountains. Mountain after mountain stared me down, their boulders stern, their exposure brutal, their climbs eternal. I was standing on the faces of giants, and I *was* a giant, with the confidence of a phoenix reborn from the fire.

Mounts Lincoln and Lafayette rose to meet me next, their crags piercing the sky. The blue blazes stayed high along the Presidential Traverse, while the white blazes stayed low, only occasionally climbing to reach peaks they found important. Along the trail were huts run by the Appalachian Mountain Club for a solid rate of $150 a bunk, no electricity or showers included. They provided warm meals, places to stay if the weather turned to shit, and chores for thru-hikers to do for dog scraps. Galehead Hut was one such hut that served hikers leftover burned pancakes and yesterday's stale oatmeal. Beggars couldn't be choosers, and who was I to pass up a free meal? Or so I thought. After I was assigned to wash the dishes, I tore into one pancake and felt the high desert of New Mexico on my tongue. Fuck it. No pancakes for me.

As I turned around to leave, a long shadow dropped over me. A voice said quietly, "Dragonsky? Hey, are you Dragonsky?"

A woman stood before me, dripping with sweat, dirt clinging to her fish belly–white legs and hands. Her gray eyes were almost completely hidden by her wafty bangs. Her expression was full, just like her rosy cheeks. A small keychain dangled from her daypack, a mini doll of sorts, or an emblem, or a good-luck charm. She was as cute as a gumdrop, and the keychain suited her.

"Yes?" I answered.

"I thought that was you! I follow you on Instagram. I can't believe you're here. I'm Transzenhiker on Instagram, but my name is Steph. I'm a trans woman. When I saw you, I knew I had to talk to you. There're not many of us out here. We have to stick together."

Something I hadn't considered when I first set out on the AT was just how impactful and important my presence was to people in the LGBTQIA community especially. Memories of Gangsigns swirled through my head. They were one of three hikers I had met over the course of the past few months who were queer. I looked at her, and then down at my hands. I did not know this woman, but somehow, to her, I was special.

"Nice to meet you, Steph, I'm Dragonsky. I really like your hiking skirt, by the way. I have a hiking dress."

Steph chuckled. "Oh, I love it! I hike in them all year long. It's very convenient."

"Do you live around here?" I asked, noting her daypack.

"I live thirty minutes from here. It's a beautiful day for a day hike. I've been climbing these mountains for over twenty years, they're quite special. How has your hike been so far?"

"Frankly, I've just fallen behind my other tramily," I confided. There was something about Steph that loosened me. "They're trying to make it to Katahdin by October first. I won't get there in time."

"When do you think you'll finish?"

"Whenever. I can always flip and go south. I have no desire to rush through it." Flipping meant starting at the ending point of Katahdin and going south instead, which was something a number of thru-hikers did. It was starting to look more and more like an option for me given that I had to contend with the deadline of Katahdin's Baxter State Park closing soon in late October for the winter.

"Well, you're doing it right, that's for sure. So many people are into the miles and not the experience."

Finally, someone who understands. My lungs expanded, and I let out a sigh.

"So, you're about to face Agiocochook next?" Steph continued.

"Huh? Ago-co-what? What's that?"

It was as if Steph had waited for me to utter the magic words. Her face was radiant, her mouth running fast.

"This land is the land of the Wabanaki, the collective name of the Maliseet, Mi'kmaq, Peskotomuhkati, and Penobscot tribes. The White Mountains is the colonist's name; the true name of this sacred land is called the Wobanadenok, the place of high white mountains. Hundreds of years ago, the white men came and tried to burn down these mountains to drive the Abenaki out. But these mountains are resilient, and they grew back even stronger. The next big climb you will face is called Agiocochook, the mountain of the great spirit. The world knows it as Mount Washington."

"How do you say it again?" I ask.

"Agi-oh-co-chook."

I repeated the word several times.

Agangiochachook. Agiakachoo. Agiohcohook.

"You will get it, Dragonsky," Steph said. Her voice brought to my mind the way that spring welcomes summer, a melodic serenity of flowers in full bloom. As she talked, the engine in my head purred with excitement. I found myself intoxicated with this new knowledge. It was as if calling the mountain by its true name allowed me to take it in with a whole new appreciation.

I asked Steph if there was anything I should keep in mind for the hike.

"It's a tough one. The weather here is the worst. People die every year. You should be fine, though, since you're a seasoned hiker. Here's my number—if you ever need anything, just call. I am retired now, so my hands are free."

The thought of being caught in a terrifying situation on the mountain floated through my mind. What death traps lay ahead? Would I fall, die of a heart attack, or freeze in place from hypothermia? Alarmed, I prodded her.

"Is that all? Are you sure I'll be fine? What else do I need to know?"

"There's a spirit on Agiocochook. May I tell you a story?"

I nodded eagerly and leaned back on my pack.

"So, I was hiking Agiocochook in February and was above the tree line on the Crawford Path in low-visibility fog. Suddenly the fog became so thick that it was a total whiteout, zero visibility. I got a case of 'whiteout vertigo' and lost all sense of proprioception.

"I fell to my knees, and in a few moments, I looked up and saw a sudden clearing and blue sky, like a giant hand was brushing aside the fog. It was then that I felt the presence of an older woman. She said I could pass now, that I had shown her my worthiness. She said she would protect me and then she affirmed to me, 'Yes, you are a woman, a worthy woman, and I believe in you.'"

Steph sighed with feeling and continued. "I had always felt mountain spirits when I hiked, but never something so concrete and real. She is my protective spirit, grandmother, and friend. She looks after me, and I try to keep her home protected. I carry a keychain on my backpack so she's always with me."

It was if the temperature had suddenly dropped. My hair stood up like a porcupine's quills. Was Steph an angel standing in front of me, except in flesh and blood? A messenger from the other realms, one whose third eye had been opened? Energy could not be created or destroyed; it could only change forms. That I truly believed and had experienced for myself many times while exploring Gettysburg and the Eastern State Penitentiary in Philadelphia. I believed her.

The mountains had a spirit, and I wanted to be intimate with them. A divine kaleidoscope had been given to me, and my eyes and soul were eager to see the unseen. Indigenous history was the key to unlocking the secrets of the mountains, I was learning, and I wanted to know how they lived, thrived, and honored the land. It suddenly dawned on me that all the miles I had walked over the past few months had been on stolen land . . . land that Indigenous people had fought to their deaths for. Now their spirits lingered here in their homes while their descendants continued to keep their traditions alive despite hundreds of years of oppression. I couldn't help but wonder if those spirits were rightfully angry about what had been stripped away from them through the massacres of colonialism, their mountains renamed after white men who referred to them as "savages." I was filled with a new insatiable hunger to face the world's smallest, deadliest mountain—Agiocochook.

Filled with gratitude, I turned to Steph for a hug.

"Thank you for all your help. I feel confident facing Agiocochook because of your story. I'm sure I'll see you again."

"I'm sure of it, too, Dragonsky. Take care and be safe up there. Remember, I am only one call away." She smiled, and we parted ways.

By the time, I reached Lakes of the Clouds Hut on September 26, 2021, it was boarded up, a ghost town at the base of Agiocochook. A huge building, once filled with hikers sharing stories with each other, gulping down piping hot soup with a view, was now awaiting the brunt of winter. One of three huts along the Presidential Traverse, this one sat over five thousand feet, 1.3 miles, from the summit of Agiocochook and had a basement called the Dungeon where hikers could stay in an emergency. I found myself along with two southbound thru-hikers within the concrete walls, evaluating the conditions that could kill us in under five minutes flat.

I'd slept in many places on the trail: an oily garage floor, on the sidewalk to the entrance to Shenandoah, on top of dozens of worms that I could feel moving under my tent floor in Vermont, but none as repulsive as this.

"What the fuck is this shit?"

There was something disturbing about the concrete box of the Dungeon. It had all the components of a jail cell. A huge black metal door with a perfectly square window and a lock bar was the entrance to this place. As if to barricade oneself in or keep others out, I was not quite sure. If I ran my hands along the cracks in the floor, my fingers would surely turn black as if dusted in soot. No bigger than a walk-in closet, it contained two sets of bunks stacked in threes. I only knew it was daylight by the slim shaft of light coming in from another window. Under it lay empty beer bottles, reminders of parties that once were.

Outside the window was a view of Agiocochook and two antennas that stuck out like bat ears, marking the visitor center, weather station, and the Mount Washington Observatory, a superb and precise monitor of weather patterns and climate changes on the high peaks. Checking it religiously was the key to survival on the mountain—it updated its forecast hourly as conditions changed drastically. During the day, I had hiked in a T-shirt and pants, but by the time I had reached the Dungeon, I had put on all my layers. The weather was forecast to be brutal, with wind gusts and chills that could sweep me away in one blow. When I went to pee outside, the urine splashed in my face, the cold so brutal that it felt like fire embers burning through my skin. The trees creaked and moaned like old rocking chairs. Staying inside was the most practical solution. Together with the two other hikers, I burrowed down in my sleeping bag, changed clothes, got out my cooking gear, and prepared to settle down for the night.

The heavy doors cracked open and a petite Asian man appeared, wearing a light wind jacket, shorts, a beanie, and a tiny daypack. His eyes grew wide as he tried to make out our figures in the dark.

"Hey guys, do you know how much longer it is to the road? I didn't know it would be this cold. I'm freezing. It was warmer earlier, I wish I had brought more clothes. Can I stay in here with you guys?"

We all gave each other that look that hikers give each other when we collectively agree that something is stupid. We were spectators, and this day hiker was the elephant in the room. Not only was it stupid but dangerous. By going into the mountains unprepared, he was in a dangerous situation that might put the lives of rescuers in jeopardy. Having empathy was complicated when yellow signage was posted not once, not twice, but three times along the trail warning hikers of death in the mountains due to weather and hypothermia.

"Do you have a sleeping bag and headlamp?" one of my companions said.

"No," the day hiker said. Thank goodness the night had come, and my facial expression blended right into the darkness. *Welp, that settles it.* Nothing could be done for this hiker. We only carried what we needed for ourselves. If he didn't get to the road fast enough, he could succumb to hypothermia, and if he stayed, he would succumb to hypothermia. All I could do was wish him well.

"You're better off moving." I gave him an apologetic look. "These mountains have killed many. You'll get hypothermic if you stay in here without gear. We can't help you."

Call me cold, but honesty was the best policy, and offering false hope would have only aggravated his situation. He let out a hard sigh and left. This was a grave situation, a serious undertaking with a high price.

"For the love of God," I muttered. I finished gnawing on a sausage to accompany my very sad bowl of noodles, telling myself that when I summited tomorrow, I'd have a beefy bowl of hot chili and hot dogs at the observatory. Food was my motivation; thoughts of food would get me through the night, up the mountain, through any feat. Any thought was better than coming to the realization that I was sleeping in a bunk that only an eight-year-old child could fit in. And not just any eight-year-old child, but an extremely agile one who could contort like a cat. If I sat up, I'd knock my head on the ceiling. The grime of the room made me feel like there were thousands of ants crawling over me. I obsessively dug my nails into my scalp, convinced there were insects and fungi in here. Clouds of vapor floated above me, the condensation dripping on my face. In desperation, I took my Klonopin, which I always carried with me for times like these. After twenty minutes, my mind settled, while the wind only ramped up. *I'll worry about that tomorrow*, I told myself.

On the morning of September 27, 2021, the Mount Washington Observatory recorded a forty-degree temperature, a twenty-degree windchill, and wind gusts of sixty-five miles per hour. Rain had been predicted, and the clouds that lingered were becoming cloudier. The jargon of the observatory confused me: How cloudy was cloudier? What the hell was I getting into? In short, this was going to be one hell of a day. But all was not lost; the promise of a one-hour window gave me the opportunity to charge full speed ahead. I shoved three bars down and looked north.

The mountain roared at me. I glanced at my phone, which read 7:15 a.m. I threw all my layers on—rain jacket, puffy, balaclava, top and bottom fleece layers, and gloves—and held my Garmin. I refused to succumb to hypothermia. Agiocochook, the highest peak in the Northeast at 6,288 feet, rarely saw clear days, and this was by no means a clear day. The crowds were nonexistent. What wild person would attempt to climb a perilous mountain in such conditions? Apparently, just me. I had stood alone in the face of a storm many times, and this time was no different. Blue sky hovered above me for an instant, as if to remind me of its fading promise. No matter how dense the murky gray clouds were, clarity was always there just beyond. The answers were there. I just needed to be still and listen to the voice within. But blue also warned of another eerie truth, the stories of hikers who played into the illusion of a flawless day. Strolling under the sun in shorts and windbreakers during the height of the day only to find themselves, hours later, perishing in the freezing fog. Such could be the case today: The weather could change in a blink of an eye. But I was prepared.

By the time I got a third of a mile up, the blue abruptly vanished and a veil of charcoal mist seemed to come out of nowhere like a poltergeist. Then came a sudden drop in temperature, as if I had walked into a hospital room. The only things that distinguished the sky from the ground were the granite rocks and stubborn shrubbery. I was in full whiteout conditions, alone. I'd been a thru-hiker for a little over a year, and this was the most awesome display of weather I'd ever experienced.

I found myself in a small quandary.

Should I continue? Should I shelter in place? How would that even work? Turning back would mean staying in the Dungeon again. I didn't have enough food for that. Seeing nothing but the silver outline of the large gothic gray cairns, I knew the only way to go was up. Turning back wasn't an option.

Within seconds, it was as if someone had flipped a switch yet again. Surrounded by an eerie quiet, I started to feel calm. Up until this point, watching the weather come in had made me almost shit my pants. Almost instinctively, I picked up my pace, taking full advantage of this "calm." *Only a quarter of a mile left.* I was clear and decisive about each move, relying on my intuition and experience to guide me. *Okay, Dragonsky, you've faced big mountains in life. You can face this one. Stay calm, damn it! Breathe! You are not lost. You know exactly where you are. You got this.*

Inside me, there was a little girl who begged to be free and face her fears. She had faced monsters her whole life. Many doubted her and didn't think she would amount to anything, but here she was now. That little Shilletha just needed to be loved, appreciated, and heard. That little girl needed me now, and we were going to summit this together. Each step represented a milestone in our lives—going to Disney World, surviving sexual abuse, enduring grief at the loss of my aunt, graduating from high school and college, being homeless in Texas, and now hiking the Appalachian Trail. Together, we could conquer anything. We'd been climbing mountains for twenty-eight years. We didn't know it then, but we knew it now.

It was if the mountain knew I was ready to challenge it. The wind suddenly howled like a jet engine ten feet above my head. Within seconds, I was being struck from the side, overtaken by a wall of violent white. Instinctively, I drove my shoulder into the wind, moving in a zigzag pattern up the mountain, chin tucked, eyes down. To make things worse, it started raining. Cold and wet were the perfect combination for hypothermia, and my thin coat could only hold for so long. My body started to tremble. I now understood how people died here. Ahead of me, something swiveled in a wide circle. Laboring up the final push, it dawned on me that I'd made it—the swiveling object was part of the weather station. Nothing I'd faced on the AT was more demanding, exhilarating, and deadly than what I had just accomplished.

The summit sign was obscured, somewhere so deep in the fog that I had to refer to my map to guide me. When I reached it, the black silhouettes of three visitors appeared, trying to get their bearings. They posed for pictures, the wind knocking them about like bowling pins.

Can y'all move? I have climbed this beast in an hour and fifteen flat. This is my victory. I just want to go inside.

Exhaustion took over me as I fumed in anger, thinking of my feat in comparison to theirs. Visitors had the option of driving up the auto road, hiking, or taking the cog train like many, if not all, had done that day, claiming they had "summited" Mount

Washington. Too bad I had missed the train coming up; I would have carried on the AT tradition of mooning the onlookers. These visitors were now raining on my perfect parade.

But did perfect really exist? And if it did, who defined it? I had never had the perfect life, even though I strived to be perfect. Whether it was mental illness or moogles coming in to rob me of my experiences, I had learned to roll with it. Depression came in cycles like the moon, yet I had the medication, therapy, and coping skills to get to another day. My depression was like nature, a force that couldn't be tamed, and it called for adaptation. I had adapted throughout my life and on the Appalachian Trail. I now had the choice to stew in my anger or accept what was and understand that nature was for everyone. Even if the moogles hadn't taken the same path as me, they had still ended up at the same spot. They had adapted to what was safest for them. I couldn't hold them to any standards of perfection. I caught myself in the middle of my judgment. Maintaining my integrity, ownership, and power over myself and owning my story was what mattered. I was only in control of my own actions, life, and destiny.

Finally, I got my chance to take a video at the sign on my GoPro, releasing my victory speech.

"So, I reached the summit of Agiocochook. Conditions are bad, but I made it. Three hundred miles or so left to Maine, about to get out of New Hampshire. It's a shitty day, but it wouldn't be the AT if it didn't throw shit at you. HELL YEAH! WHOOOOOOOOOO!"

I entered the Summit Information Center, which appeared to be more of an amusement park than an "informational center."

People were everywhere, wandering into the shops to buy their prized mementos, stuffing their faces at the café. My hunger overcame me, and I bought two hot dogs, string cheese, and a piping hot chocolate and collected myself at a table next to a heater. I removed all my wet layers, laying them near the heater to dry. With the weather becoming increasingly volatile, I contemplated my next move. How would I get the hell off the mountain? Technically I would still need to descend to complete the trail. It was the first time on trail when I considered capitulating to the weather for safety reasons. Risking my life for mountains was not who I was. Coming down alive was paramount; coming down in a body bag was unfavorable, to say the least. Back and forth, I paced in my head as I contemplated my decision.

Am I a failure?

Should I just risk it all?

If I took a shuttle, that meant I would have to return to descend the mountain on a later date if I wanted to say that I had completed all 2,193 miles of the Appalachian Trail. Honesty was what I held myself to; I was not a liar. In a panic, I pulled up my phone and started googling the ATC, sweat dripping from my forehead. I knew that they allowed two hundred miles skipped due to weather and trail closures and still validated such thru-hikes. Even so, I was committed to coming back to Agiocochook to finish the descent after I completed Maine. The purity of the trail was at stake.

The hike that I was dreaming of was becoming a nightmare I wanted to avoid. Anxiety swooped in like a lightning storm, blowing the power out, leaving me to panic in the dark. Tears welled up in my eyes. Why didn't things ever go my way? Instead of completing the AT on Katahdin and returning home afterward, I'd have to flip back to return to Agiocochook. At least I'd be returning to a land that I loved unconditionally. That wasn't a bad thing. Detours had always been a part of my life experience, and so if this was the way it had to go, so be it. *Traditional* was never a label I took on; there was simply nothing traditional about my life. As a child, I had been neglected, abused, mistreated, and unheard. Now I owned who I was, a Black lesbian woman thru-hiking the trail with severe depression and anxiety. I had defeated the odds that I would "amount to nothing."

Ready to embrace the adventure before me with a new plan, I became content. The mountain would always be there, waiting for me to stand on her mighty head once again. One, two, three hours passed before I made my decision to descend via shuttle for a solid price of fifty bucks plus tip. To pass time before the shuttle's departure, I ventured around the entrance and found a list of all the people who had died on the mountain. Hypothermia was not the only killer; it was also avalanches, heart attacks, and falling and vanishing into the freezing fog, never to see the light of day again. Their sun had set, but for me, it was the dawn of a new day. Almost as soon as we departed from the summit, the wind ceased, the dense fog lifted, and the world became calm. Suddenly, I could see the world below. The sun shone with all her splendor against a backdrop of blue, the crags of the Whites boasting proudly in the sky.

I looked up at what I had just accomplished, and in my heart I felt the flutter of a hummingbird's wings. There was nothing that

I couldn't achieve on my own. Being in the storm had taught me that I wanted to live more than ever. I could have easily given up, sat down, and let nature smite me. Depression wanted me to die, but hiking taught me that I wanted to live. If not for the mountains, then for myself.

16

NEW MOON ON KATAHDIN (MAINE)

"No Rain, No Pain, No Maine" has always been the slogan of the AT, and I hit all three marks. I had endured the downpours of the Smoky Mountains in Tennessee and North Carolina, the pain of blackflies biting my legs and thigh-deep mud in Vermont, and now, before me, my last state line. A sign that read 282 MILES TO KATAHDIN. 1908 TO SPRINGER MOUNTAIN.

I embraced the sign as if I were hugging a long-lost friend. I started recording the moment, tears flowing down my face.

"This is my last state line. Holy shit. The New Hampshire–Maine state line. These last one hundred miles were hard. No one can ever prepare you for this feeling. I'm so emotional."

Maine was known for its remote wilderness—about 90 percent of Maine is forested, the highest percentage of any state. According to everything I'd read about it, this state was the most beloved by thru-hikers. I couldn't fathom this. Maine made New Hampshire look like child's play, a warmup to the actual game.

Bitching through Maine was my specialty, and I left no crumbs. In photographs Maine looks deceptive, displaying serene autumn colors, crystal clear lakes, and endless mountains. And it had all that. However, it also contained everything that I hated except Katahdin and the Hundred-Mile Wilderness. To start, giant slabs of stone and boulders known as the Mahoosuc Notch tried to kill you in a boulder field between two mountains, infamously known as the toughest mile of the AT. Just imagine getting to Maine and risking twisting your ankle or dislocating your shoulder by falling into a crevasse. The size of those boulders ranged from small washing machines to compact cars, all presenting themselves like a puzzle, necessary to crawl over, under, sideways—crab-walking—to figure one's way out. And if that wasn't enough, there was Mahoosuc Arm, the mountain you had to climb after. Why the fuck did the Notch need an appendage? Someone truly hated hikers. Someone truly hated me.

I ate shit and fell into one of those nasty crevasses. I had approached a boulder and assumed I had cleared it with a jump, failing to recognize there was no solid landing on the other side. My feet dangled for a millisecond before I plummeted to the ground. The only thing that saved me from breaking anything was my pack, which had gotten wedged between the boulders. Shaken, I stood up, blood dripping from my knees.

Fucking Christ! I can't do this alone! This is dangerous. Why aren't there others around? At this rate, I won't make it.

Taking a moment to catch my breath, I checked the date. It was the first of October, the day Funghi planned to summit Katahdin. An image quickly entered my mind of Funghi standing at the sign, screaming into the air. Good for her. Accepting what I couldn't change gave me peace. At the end of the day, I could only be responsible for myself. It was nice to be back on my own, going at my own pace, taking as many breaks as I needed and camping wherever I wanted. Summiting Katahdin on my own birthday, October 19, was my goal, and it would be the best gift to myself. However, time was not on my side. Baxter State Park, where Katahdin lived, could be closed by then, barring me from summiting. Snow was the great humbler, the ultimate deity, with the power to close roads and trails to protect the environment and the safety of hikers. There was no telling when it would close; it could snow tomorrow. Hell, I wasn't a fortune teller with a magic crystal ball. Nature was a ticking time bomb, and all I could do was adapt. Getting upset over it changed nothing. I didn't want to flip—but the fact was I needed to.

It was time to pull a favor and call Steph.

"Hey, Steph, I was wondering if you could help drive me somewhere? Baxter State Park might close soon, and I think I want to flip and go southbound. I don't want to rush, but I also don't want to miss Katahdin. . . ."

I braced myself, expecting a no, the ask too big. I feared rejection. Throughout the trail, I had asked for help time and time again. I carried the shame of "wanting too much" or "being selfish." But the

Appalachian Trail had provided so much good among the bad. It was a constant give-and-take, like the tides. There were those who had helped me in Tennessee and Pennsylvania and those who had robbed me like Connor in Virginia. Those negative interactions only made me lean into my intuition more. Ultimately, I chose to believe that kindness and love triumphed over racism and hate; I chose to be brave and to trust again. My wish to be loved and to not be alone meant I only wanted to see the good in people, and so I believed that everything would work out. I was the manifester of my own destiny.

"You got it," came Steph's voice over the phone. "Let's work out a plan. I can be there on the third and drive you up. It's not a problem."

I let my pack fall from my back, onto the ground. Glassy-eyed, I stuck my finger in my ear, pretending to scoop out wax as if I couldn't hear her. Was she serious? She would be coming from New Hampshire.

"Are you sure? Do you need gas or—"

"I don't want anything. Just remember me when you're famous. Take me out to dinner or something. I don't want your money. I want to help you on your journey in any way that I can. Like I said, I'm retired. Where are you going to be on the third?"

"Andover, Maine. There's a hostel called the Pine Ellis. I'll wait there for you. Thank you so much, Steph."

"Always, Dragonsky. See you soon."

That was the power of trust, the belief that, for once, good things could come to me.

And so, on October 3, Steph came by, swooped me up, and drove me three and a half hours into the boundless woods of Baxter State Park for my trek up to Katahdin. She dropped me off at the camp store at Abol Bridge, where other hikers were already gathered. In the background, Katahdin basked in a sea of autumn colors, wide across the horizon, like a volcano with a flattop.

"If you need me to come get you, just let me know. I'm a phone call away. You got this, Dragonsky," Steph said.

"Will do, Steph. Please let me know when you make it home. Not like I'll see it on my phone—service seems spotty out here—but, ya know, for when I get into town!"

I waved as my angel drove off, my heart full.

Baxter's motto is "Wilderness first, recreation second," and the rules and regulations are strict and enforced with costly fines. Katahdin, or the "Greatest Mountain," belongs to the Penobscot Nation, and Baxter goes to great lengths to make sure it is protected. Not just anyone can camp or hike through the park; there are a series of steps. The first order of business is to register at a sign-up kiosk by the Abol Bridge to stay at a campground called the Birches. It is the best campsite for thru-hikers due to proximity to the trailhead. Three spots remained on the white sheet, and I signed my full name as *Shilletha Curtis "Dragonsky"* and wrote the date. It looked like I'd be summiting October 5. I made my way to camp, ate a cup of noodles, and got set up. That night, I joined a few other hikers under the stars as they pondered the completion of their journey.

"I'm just ready to get it done with. I'm so tired," said one.

"I don't want to thru-hike ever again," said another.

Finally, one hiker had something positive to say. All hope was not lost.

"I'm glad that I did it. This was a hard trail, but I want to do the Pacific Crest Trail next. I'm going to miss being hiker trash. Miss not worrying about any responsibilities. I don't want to go back to work." She turned to me. "How about you, Dragonsky?"

"Oh, I'm flipping and heading southbound to finish up by Andover. I also didn't get to descend Agiocochook—"

They looked at each other, shrugging.

"—I mean Mount Washington, because of the fog. I didn't want to get lost and die. I'll have to go back to the Whites to finish after. For me, this is the start of a new adventure. It's not the ending I wanted, but it's the ending I got. I've made my peace with it."

And with that, I went to bed.

Forgetting to set my alarm, my morning started off in a frenzy. Today, at least, I got to pack light. The ranger handed us bags to put our gear in, to collect at the end of the day, allowing me to bring only my nearly empty pack, complete with just water, snacks, a headlamp, and my puffy coat. It was already nine a.m. by the time I gobbled down four packs of instant oatmeal and a liter of water. As I went on my way, my body felt off. Something had not settled nicely in my stomach. Within reach of the ranger station to collect my permit, I knelt over, wincing in pain. Back and forth I paced like a tiger in a cage, not knowing whether to go back to camp or to go forward on the trail. Well, my body decided for me. I dashed into the woods, still within sight of onlookers, and released my bowels.

Relieved that now I could *finally* get started, I placed my gear at the designated drop location when a foul smell of dog shit invaded my nostrils. For the life of me, I couldn't figure out where it was coming from. Until I did. Looking down at my boots, I saw streaks of brown. *Why me? Why today?* I searched for any stick I could find to rid my boots of the poop, scraping like a wild woman, but time was ticking.

Fuck it. I must get to that station.

I dashed to the station, sweat pouring from my underarms.

"Ah, do I still have time? If I need more time, can I extend my campsite?" I asked the ranger as I filled out the card. I paused when I came to the question asking me to mark if I was northbound, southbound, or a flip-flop. What was I? Since February I had hiked north toward Katahdin, but now my hike had changed. To say I was a flip-flopper meant I had flipped the whole way out of order, when in fact I had hiked nearly all thirteen states consistently north. Marking it as northbound felt more genuine.

"No. Nothing I can do here. You got a late start. You walked here from Georgia, I'm sure you can get up and over in three hours or less. Everyone else can."

Excuse me? I snapped my head back. His tone was rough like an angry New Yorker caught in rush hour traffic. Flat and cold. No sympathy, and very ableist.

"Um, actually I can't. I have a back injury that prevents me from moving at lighting speed."

His lips stayed firm. I handed him the sheet.

"You're missing a direction. Which way did you go?"

"I started in Georgia and got to Maine, and then I flipped—"

"You're a flip-flopper, then."

"No, I'm not, I—you know what?"

I circled the northbound direction, threw him the sheet, and continued my trek.

"Fucking dick," I whispered under my breath.

The climb was not arduous so much as it was serene. The leaves danced around me, falling from their high branches to the ground, leaving a carpet of cranberry-red and pumpkin-orange leaves. I picked one up and tucked it into my ponytail. Autumn was the grand finale of a fruitful season, one of change and acceptance. I might have started in winter when the forest was dead and cold, but I was ending in autumn, a season of transformation. I was used to the cycle of the seasons, which mimicked my lifelong cycle of mental illness—a continuum of growth, relapse, recovery, and change.

Katahdin Falls was my soundtrack for the first mile, her pristine waters beckoning me to drink from them unfiltered, and so I did. Like an animal, on all fours, I dunked my head in. When I'd had my fill, I continued to the next section of Katahdin—a series of rebar and freehand bouldering. Spider-Man would have thrived here; it was like scaling the sides of buildings. This adventure was not for the faint of heart, as three day hikers soon found out. Above me, a teenage girl clung to the rebar, unsure of how to get to the next handhold above her. If the rebar had been frail, she could have certainly broken it from trembling too much. Her mother was below her, sending encouragement.

"Honey! Honey, you have to place your foot to the right. Use your legs, hun! You can do it! We will come after you. We will be right there."

I found this odd. The poor little thing was just a kid, and she had not a damn clue of what to do. Observing this, I made my way over to attempt the section.

"Hey, are you a thru-hiker?" the mother said.

"Yes, I am. I—"

"SEE? We have a pro right here. Watch, she's going to show us how to do it! She's going to make it look so easy." She looked at me as if I were an Olympian about to perform some tumbling routine.

Lovely. I hate being on the spot. I grabbed the rebar and pulled myself up with one hand, using my strong legs to support me.

"SEE! I TOLD YOU, HUN!"

The young girl looked at me. "This is my first hike ever. I guess it doesn't help that I'm afraid of heights."

Wow. Go figure.

"Well, you chose a hell of a hike to do for your first one. It's okay, I am scared of heights sometimes, too," I said reassuringly, giving her a smile that said, *You're not alone.* As I continued on, the image of them faded away into the background, even if their voices didn't.

"Hey, hun, if we have been here for this long, I don't think we're going to make it. It's already three thirty p.m. We still have, what, about two to three miles to go? Let's start heading down."

Good decision.

For the next few hours, I bouldered over rocks and crevasses and climbed ladders while making sure I snacked. Finally, close to the top, I could already see the famous sign, a wooden board with words engraved in it, marking the northern terminus of the Appalachian Trail. With only a third of a mile to go, I prepped my GoPro. To the right of Katahdin was a gnarly ridge with sheer drops on each side known as the Knife Edge. Apparently over forty people had fallen to their death attempting it. Now, *that* was more of an adventure to me than Katahdin. Death was still a lure to me, like bait to a fish. The greater the risk, the harder the fall, and with my depression I could lose it all in a split second. Suicidal thoughts flitted in my mind for a brief second. My mind was fragile, the Knife Edge a catalyst for my dangerous thoughts. Who knew a mountain could trigger this? But that was mental illness, even at Katahdin, even in good times when I was happy. Depression knows how to sneak in through the cracks.

The mountains give and the mountains take away. Just keep breathing, I said to myself, inhaling a gulp of fresh alpine air.

I stood in the great expanse, not a cloud or human around. Like every hiker, I wanted my picture taken on Katahdin. But this wasn't what I expected—a sleeping mountain. Wasn't Katahdin everyone's favorite hike? Or maybe everyone had already descended, and I was too slow. Like always.

Out of the blue came a voice I recognized. It was Sunshine, a hiker I had passed a few times on trail. She knew of me from Instagram; she was a Dragonfly.

"Well, looka here. There she is! The badass hiker, Dragonsky. You're lookin' a little lost. Ya okay there?"

"I got all the way up here, and there's not a damn person in sight. I want to take a picture at the top. . . ."

"Yo, don't even worry about it. I got you. I was just about to offer. I'm on my way down, but I'll follow you up. Let's get 'er done."

"Thank you, truly. That means a lot!"

With my GoPro in hand, I started recording, Sunshine behind me.

"Very emotional going up to the sign. Oh my god, I am going to cry. I can't believe this is happening, and my friend is going to take my picture. Feels, feels, feels!"

With each step, the rocks crunched under my feet, and sweat doused my body as if I'd been swimming. I was wearing a purple sports bra and navy-blue shorts that no longer hugged my body tightly, with a red leaf in my ponytail.

Treading on the sea of rocks, I made my way over to the sign, placed my pack on the ground, and admired the mountains surrounding me. Then I stood face-to-face with the sign, an arm's distance away, reluctant to touch it. Placing my hand on my head, I paused for a minute, reflecting on my journey. Katahdin was everyone else's perfect ending. It sure as hell wasn't mine. As I placed my two hands on the plaque, my chin tucked into my chest, trying to force out tears that weren't there, I wondered what my true ending was. Where it would be. If I even had an ending to the AT trail or the larger life path that I would have to walk on whenever I left the mountains to return to the fictional real world. The *true* real world was here, in the forest, on top of the mountains, a place where I belonged. Where I could be myself and love myself unapologetically. When I lifted my head up, I looked into the camera. Sunshine was recording me.

"Was it worth it?" she said.

"Definitely worth it." I chuckled anxiously, squinting my eyes, hoping that tears would come. They never did. Instead, all I could do was laugh.

"Springer is so far away now. I am here. I have done this," I said for the camera, pounding my fists on the plaque in sync with my words. I threw up the peace sign as I turned my back to the sign for the final time.

Goodbye, Katahdin. Here's to the start of a new adventure. It was time to turn around and tackle the Hundred-Mile Wilderness and the trek back to Andover, Maine.

Millinocket, a trail town situated twenty-five miles from Katahdin Streams campground by the Birches, offered shuttles back to town. Trail towns in Maine were adorably quaint, lined with colorful houses, dispensaries, and white people. Millinocket was no exception. It was a town you could cruise through and not even realize you'd been through the heart of it. The only iconic marker was Katahdin's autumn veil, her presence dominating the sky in the far distance. One main street ran through the town, and on both sides there were a few bars, restaurants, churches, and stores. Without Katahdin and Baxter State Park, it would probably have been the town that the world forgot, surrounded by thousands of acres of forests, rivers, and lakes in the middle of East Bumblefuck. That was Maine, remote and wild. And who could afford that? Who had access to that? White people.

I stayed at the Appalachian Trail Hostel and Outfitters, run by former thru-hikers for thru-hikers. At the hostel, thru-hikers celebrated the completion of their thru-hikes by sleeping and drinking. Although my hike wasn't ending, I figured a little partying couldn't hurt. I ventured into the bars alone. Bad idea. My skin was still black in a state that was 94.2 percent white.

The patrons of the bar consisted almost entirely of middle-aged and older white men. Most of them appeared to have never seen a Black woman before. Entering the room, I felt like an intruder, a robber with a ski mask, a curiosity and also a threat. Every pair of eyes laid themselves on me, and I couldn't stay still. Wrapping my locs around my finger, my stomach formed knots. I let out a laugh, but my smile was narrow and uncomfortable.

Why am I here? Why are they looking at me like I'm an animal at a zoo? But I'd just summited Katahdin. I was close to completing the AT. Damn it, I deserved to be wherever I wanted.

Get it together, Dragonsky, I told myself. *You've survived the worst. You didn't just survive to get here; you struggled, cried, and prevailed, and you looked fear in the face. You grabbed life by the ovaries. You got through the Mason–Dixon Line. Maybe they will be receptive to you. You deserve to take up space.*

My mind was going a million hours an hour. Was I being too judgmental? No, no, I was being cautious. I remembered Connor. *Test out the waters, and if anything goes sour, leave. Just fucking go.*

Don't let white men steal your joy. Do not let these motherfuckers win.

I lifted my head high, stuck my chest out, and approached the only empty stool left in the bar, beside two white men.

"Hey, do you mind if I sit here?"

"You *sure* can," he said, then he raised his voice. "You definitely can, pretty lady."

He was silent for a moment, as if making some crucial assessment to ensure that I had passed inspection. I kept my face blank.

"Well, thanks, I appreciate it. Seems like it's packed tonight."

"My name is Bill, and this here next to me is Tom. Tom! Move over for the lady!"

Tom was shorter than Bill and carried his weight like a weapon, while Tom was lanky and long. Both had long beards like Santa Claus and wore matching green hunting caps. They reeked of alcohol.

"Tom, say hi to this pretty young lady sittin' next to us, will ya, and get 'er a drink?"

"Hi, young lady. What's your name?" said Tom.

"Uh . . . Dragonsky."

"Right. I'm Tom." His eyes slid back down to his phone.

Bill looked back at me and continued. "You thru-hiking the Appalachian Trail? We've had a bunch of hikers come by. It's about that time, I suppose. You made it to the best town in Maine. We're all a bunch of friendly folks."

Leaning into my silence, he continued, "We don't see a lot of your folks out here. You're very exotic-looking, a very pretty lady."

Exotic? "What?" I said this time, unable to stay silent. Bill turned around, handed me a beer, and snickered. His face was beet red.

I'd been called a nigger before, but not exotic. Never in my twenty-eight years of life had I ever been referred to as exotic. *Who says that? What do these white men think of me, that I'm a motherfucking animal?* Suddenly I felt shame. I lowered my eyes, my locs dangling in front of them.

"Excuse me, what does that mean?" I repeated. The shock made my spinal cord feel like it was detaching from my body. I had thought New England would be liberal, that Maine would be welcoming. It was Vacationland. I was sure that Millinocket had its fair share of visitors, with Katahdin as its signature icon. I wrapped my arms around my stomach, rocking back and forth. Would I shit myself or throw up?

"I'm sorry for my friend," said Tom. "He's just a little drunk. He's just being nice, ya know." He grinned widely.

I tried to rationalize his words in my head. Maybe it was a joke. Maybe I hadn't heard right. But the truth was there was never any rationalization for racism. How did you rationalize hate, white supremacy, and injustice? You didn't. Instead, I had been taught to just endure, to not engage. If I did, I could end up lifeless on the side of a road in a ditch.

"It's just that you're unique," Bill pressed on. "I'd love to take you home and show you more of Millinocket—take you huntin', kill some bucks." He pulled out his phone, plonking his arm down on the table. "Here is one I shot a month ago. He was a big ole boy."

I looked at my knees, pretending to take a glance. "Cool."

I couldn't stomach looking at his phone. First the racism, the justification for it, and now he was showing me a dead deer. Dead animals being held up by men were repulsive to me. *Why is this the thing to brag about? It's great that that brings you joy, bro, but could you ask before you show me that? Can this possibly get any worse?*

As if on cue, he reached his hand out. "Can I touch your hair?" His outstretched hand brushed my locs, grabbing one in his fist.

I jerked my head back, confused and disgusted. *Not today, Satan.* Never in America had a white man touched my hair, or even dared to ask. The only thing more offensive than asking a Black woman if you can touch her hair is proceeding to touch it without permission. I had never asked my white friends if I could touch their hair. By touching my hair, he was sending a deeper message to me: that white hair was normal and my hair was other. That we were not equal, and we would never be. Until people like him stopped seeing people like me as other or less than, the system of whiteness and racism would continue to thrive.

I felt like a dog that had been poked and prodded, waiting to lash out at any time. That was what they wanted. It put me in a position where I either felt obligated to go with the flow or could respond accordingly and be labeled an angry, unruly, difficult Black woman—stereotypes assigned to me at birth. My Nigerian, Ghanaian, Congolese, and Cameroonian blood boiled, reminding me of the horrors my ancestors had endured. This wasn't the first time Africa-derived bodies were seen as artifacts for white people.

Ota Benga, born in Congo in 1883, was brought to the United States in 1904 by avowed white supremacist and former African missionary Samuel Phillips Verner, who was under a contract with the Louisiana Purchase to bring "pygmies" back home to be part of a human exhibition. In 1906, nearly a quarter million New Yorkers flocked to see the so-called "pygmy" on exhibit in the Monkey House at the Bronx Zoo in New York City, where Ota often sat on a stool in silence, mocked the crowds, and played with the orangutan that shared his cage. This dehumanization took a toll on Ota, and he later shot himself in the heart at just thirty-three years old.

And here I now was, a hundred years later, sitting in a bar on display for white men to see and touch. Sickened, the bile burning in my throat, I got up and left. The battle was lost. I put my sword down and walked away. I would not allow myself to be treated like this.

This was America. At the core of it was deeply ingrained racism. This country had never been built for us, even though Africa-derived people had helped to build it alongside Indigenous peoples. Maine was a rude wake-up call, reminding me of how white-dominated the trail and outdoor spaces actually were. The sense of being out of place, as a Black woman, was something I had always felt in America, but now I felt its true sting. Katahdin is seen as the perfect ending by almost every thru-hiker, and Maine as the most beautiful state, but to me, in that moment, nothing could have been uglier.

It was only in the Hundred-Mile Wilderness that I felt any love for Maine. The most remote section of trail was a stunning oasis of crystal clear lakes, attracting the animal that had called out to me at Disney World as a little girl, the animal I was named after. Dragonflies danced across the surface, their presence reassuring me that I wasn't alone. Whenever they were near, it was confirmation that I was on the right path. Anytime I felt down, depressed, or scared, they lingered or hovered in front of me. One even perched next to me as I was eating my breakfast, as if to say, *I got you*. I couldn't help but wonder if my aunt had come to me in the form of the dragonfly. Each time I saw them, I felt that security and love that she gave to me. Unconditional love. A warmth bubbled up in my heart like a shaken bottle of soda.

Dragonflies reminded me to slow down, to appreciate the beauty of the present moment, and to embrace change. And that I did. Because I had flip-flopped, and the terrain was mostly flat, I took my dear sweet time, relishing in the colors of autumn. I hardly saw anyone—not any northbound thru-hikers charging to the finish line or even others like me who had flipped because of injury, time, or weather. This was a place where I waded through rivers and lagoons on foot, the water waist deep in some places, without pulleys or ropes to hang on to for support, forcing me to rely only on my intuition and trekking poles for stability. Each crossing felt symbolic for me, like a cleansing, a connection to my African roots, symbolizing my overcoming great obstacles after being forcefully misplaced here on American soil. The odds had been stacked against me, or so they said. I wasn't born to win. Yet on the other side of the river was freedom, liberation, and a new revelation. Every river I waded through, I was one step closer to Agiocochook and the land of the great spirit in New Hampshire, one step closer to completing the AT.

There was one thing I couldn't leave behind as I made my way back to Andover while winter unleashed its fury on Maine: mental illness. From the Bigelow Mountain Range to the mighty Kennebec River, over hard trail, rocks, and slick roots, while collecting bruises, scratches, and cuts, depression still lurked in my mind. But this time, something felt different.

For so many years I had just wanted to survive, to get through. But the Appalachian Trail was changing me, and I was starting to think about the future. What would I thru-hike next? My dream, at first a tiny stream, was now rushing into a mighty river. There was a crown that I sought that only one Black woman and one Black man had achieved prior—and that was the Triple Crown of hiking: the Appalachian Trail, the Continental Divide Trail, and the Pacific Crest Trail. My heart was set: I was going to be the second Black woman to achieve the Triple Crown.

But even that alone couldn't fully answer the larger question of my life. How would I cope after I took my final steps on the trail, any trail? Who was I now as an individual both on and off the mountains? Thru-hiking was that happy place in my life. A place where I could be myself, *with* severe depression, anxiety, and ADHD, and be accepted by nature, a loving force that did not judge. It was only humans who judged, ridiculed, and abandoned me. The mountains were a place where I could stand on my own two feet and forgive the little girl inside me. It wasn't her fault her aunt died. It wasn't her fault that she had to survive. She deserved so much more. She deserved to be heard, and I finally heard her. Her name was Shilletha, and she had never known that, one day, Dragonsky would give her freedom. She had never known that she could be happy.

Hate could not prevail because all that was inside me was love. Despite the abuse that could have turned me into a monster, there was a light inside, dimmed but still burning, waiting to grow brighter.

Mental illness and racism had tried to take me out, bringing me to my tipping point, nearly costing me my life. But every day, I soldiered on to keep hiking, to look depression and racism in the face. To accept the things I couldn't change about myself and love myself fully. To own who I was and unapologetically walk in my truth. That had been my promise to my aunt. She had never gotten the chance to meet Dragonsky, but she had always believed that I could stand on mountains. She was right, but I didn't want to just stand on mountains; I wanted to make them quiver in their bones.

Sometimes depression hurt so much that I felt I was going to break. Little by little, depression and suicidal thoughts could chip away at me until I nearly crumbled. Like the moon, mental illness is a continuous cycle, one that waxes and wanes from light to dark and dark to light. I carried that darkness through the trail in a heavy pack, one that weighed me down but also made me stronger. And when I came out from the other side of New Hampshire, standing on the summit of Mount Adams with Steph and a friend of hers, I felt whole, free, and alive.

"You're a force on the mountain," Steph said.

A force on the mountain was exactly what I was. My heart beat harder and more fiercely than it ever had before.

We attempted to get back to Agiocochook to descend, but once again the mountains said no. The winter and snow prevented it. And that was okay. Next up on my list was the Continental Divide Trail from Mexico to Canada, and I knew I'd be back after to finish what I couldn't now with Steph while her spirit friend watched over us. My whole life I'd been climbing mountains—literal and metaphorical—and they had broken me down and built me back up. Just like how years of tectonic plates smashing into each other created new forms from the chaos. The mountains stood strong in the middle of everything nature threw at them. And among those mountains, a warrior claimed her throne. The dragonflies named her Dragonsky, a lesbian Nigerian woman who found herself on the AT and who would continue to find herself on the trails for the rest of her life.

I finally knew how strong I really was. Standing on the mountains, in the Wobanadenok, it was time to release Shilletha and remove the burdens of her pack. For once in my life, I could finally pack light.

ACKNOWLEDGMENTS

Super love and thanks to my agent and team at Andscape for always believing in me and my project. Lynn Johnston has been truly phenomenal, patient, and understanding. I am honored to have such a fierce and passionate agent who truly believes in my book and meets me where I am. Thank you for listening and working with me and my vision. Without you, I would not be here.

Aliya King Neil—wow, you have inspired me beyond my imagination. Thank you for your time and patience and advocating for me. Representation matters. Thank you, Olivia Zavitson, for making everything run smoother and less stressful all around, and to my amazing publishing team, including Jennifer Levesque, Tonya Agurto, Ann Day, Daneen Goodwin, Steph Sumulong, Amy King, Guy Cunningham, Meredith Jones, and Raina Kelley. I can't believe I get to work with such an impressive group.

Without the guidance of Kimberley Lim, I would have gotten lost turning my words into a book. Your expertise is only outmatched by your care and empathy. L Renee, aka urbanclimbr, took incredible shots of me for the book jacket that made me feel completely special.

Thank you, Appalachian Trail Conservancy, Arc'teryx, and Superfeet, for your sponsorships and unwavering support.

I'm indebted to Tara Sullivan for editing my first drafts. Thank you to Jennifer Pastiloff and Jesica Sweedler DeHart for reading my book and seeing the beauty and worth in it.

Thank you to my friends back at home who sent resupply boxes when I needed food—Liz, Leilah, Megan, Meggen, Meghan, Maureen, and my phenomenal cousin Kesia. You came through when it counted most.

Thank you to my aunt and uncle for raising an amazing human. They made me who I am.

And last I want to thank my Dragonflies, trail angels, and anyone who championed me and my journey. You made a difference.